UNRAVELING THE SPIDER'S NET

UNRAVELING THE SPIDER'S NET

A Family's Struggle with Epilepsy, Parkinson's Disease, and Depression

Nancy Carlisle Schumacher

February 1, 2005 - November 28, 2009

Copyright © 2010 by Nancy Carlisle Schumacher.

ISBN: Hardcover   978-1-4500-1104-4
           Softcover   978-1-4500-1103-7

All rights reserved. No part of this book may be reproduced or transmitted in any form or by any means, electronic or mechanical, including photocopying, recording, or by any information storage and retrieval system, without permission in writing from the copyright owner.

This book was printed in the United States of America.

To order additional copies of this book, contact:
Xlibris Corporation
1-888-795-4274
www.Xlibris.com
Orders@Xlibris.com

CONTENTS

Section I: 1995-1997

Chapter I	Emilia and Marriage	13

Section II: March 1997-June 1998

Chapter II	Yale/1997	21
Chapter III	Leah returns to New Haven	23
Chapter IV	Daniel Dies, Travel in Europe	27

Section III: 2000-2002

Chapter V	Problems in writing/painting in France	33
Chapter VI	Emilia continues at SCSU/Moona goes to Texas	37
Chapter VII	George begins to court Emilia	40

Section IV: April 2004-June 2004

Chapter VIII	Alex dies/Moona, Leah and Emilia go to Houston	51
Chapter IX	May 2004	63
Chapter X	Graduation/ Trip to France/New book	66

Section V: July19 2004-October 1, 2004

Chapter XI	Bumming around on Emilia's Turf	71
Chapter XII	Emilia works	77

Chapter XIII	Labor Day	81
Chapter XIV	George first visits the VA Hospital/ Trouble with Chris	83
Chapter XV	George and Emilia go to the VA hospital and talk with Bary about marriage	88

Section VI: October-December 2004

Chapter XVI	Hallucinations begin	93
Chapter XVII	Emilia hangs pictures at *Claire's*	*98*
Chapter XVIII	VA Hospital's ER/Neurologist	103
Chapter XIX	George and Emilia get married	108
Chapter XX	George stops sleeping in bed and sleeps on the couch. He can not sleep under covers	111
Chapter XXI	Emilia travels to New Orleans and Austin	114
Chapter XXII	Emilia returns to Connecticut	118
Chapter XXIII	George falls	120
Chapter XXIV	George has hip surgery at Saint Raphael's	129
Chapter XXV	Hip surgery I and II	131

Section VII: January 2005

Chapter XXVI	Emilia takes George to the Orthopedist; she grows ill	137
Chapter XXVII	Emilia paints while she is ill	141

Section VIII: February 2005

Chapter XXVIII	George's will and his will power	145

Section IX: March 2005

Chapter XXIX	Emilia approaches the social worker about the reunion, Nicole and George talk about Alex	153

Chapter XXX	George begins to look worse, has his medicine changed, and takes less interest in Emilia	159
Chapter XXXI	Easter 2005	163
Chapter XXXII	Silver Valley Nursing Home and Insurance	165
Chapter XXXIII	August 2005	172
Chapter XXXIV	The Mortgage and the Divorce	174
Chapter XXXV	Emilia turns over the Power of Attorney to Nicole; Emilia starts going to SCSU for her masters in Public Health. Reba still asks for money	176

Section X: Summer, 2006

Chapter XXXVI	Emilia is invited to Helsinki by Amir. Her marriage is annulled. She completes the edit on the epidemiology book, has a book returned, and publishes a new book	183

Section XI: 2007-2008

Chapter XXXVII	Emilia goes to Singapore	193
Chapter XXXVIII	Emilia goes to Boston to end it with Reba	195
Chapter XXXIX	George dies	203
Chapter XL	Bankruptcy, school, and generic medication Fall of 2008	207
Chapter XLI	Financial Winter Worries	216

Section XII: 2009

Chapter XLII	Emilia sees doctor, has tests, studies and falls on ice	223
Chapter XLIII	Moona considers her pregnancy and Isaiah. Emilia entertains guests and works	228

This book is dedicated to my children and friends
who have made the recounting of these tales possible.

Special thanks are given to Joy Scott
whose editing has been especially appreciated.

Nancy Carlisle Thornton Schumacher

Section I:

1995-1997

Chapter I

Emilia and Marriage

    Although Emilia had moved away from Minnesota to elude her ex-husband's advances, she hadn't recognized how much control he had retained over her thoughts and actions. Daniel, the man whom she loved and had come east to pursue, seemed detached from her, and yet she knew that he cared for her deeply. At that time, she had no idea how quickly the Parkinson's was progressing in his body. She was still learning about the disease, and had no idea how difficult it would be to lose someone to Parkinson's disease. Although her uncle Conda had died of the disease, she hadn't been around him when he was ill. She had several of his letters showing how his writing had deteriorated until it was illegible; then they stopped completely. Uncle Conda had enjoyed writing and he had always written to her and her three daughters, calling them 'his little rainbows'. The girls had never forgotten the love that he had shown them. Daniel had been concerned about her children also, and always asked about them. That was something that their father, George, rarely did.
    Emilia had continued to write and paint when she arrived in New Haven. Waiting for love was difficult. Although Daniel was glad to see her, he wasn't as attentive as she had expected him to be. He came over for lunch once in September, and upon leaving told her that they should meet again every two weeks. Then she heard nothing for two months except that he was busy and away. When she had first arrived, she had noticed that his body was more rigid than it had been two years earlier. He could no longer hide the tremor in his hand. To Emilia, who had dealt with a fractured hip since 1961 and epilepsy since 1940, Parkinson's didn't

seem to be insurmountable. Now that she was living in New Haven, he called her less frequently than he had when she was in Minnesota. She knew that he was busy, and that Parkinson's disease was affecting him adversely. When he took her out to dinner, she noticed the tremor in his hands. But she had been heartened by his attention to her when she told him that Nicole and Moona would be visiting in December.

"We'll have to plan something special for them," he had said. "Do they like theatre?"

"Yes," Emilia answered.

"I'll get tickets for 'Cats' which is opening at the Schubert Theatre in December."

"That would be wonderful."

After lunch, he had told her that the following year would bring changes. She soon found out that this meant that he would be retiring and avoiding people. He procured the tickets for Nicole, Moona and Emilia, but was absent from the performance. Before they left to return to Minnesota, he took them to the Union Club. Daniel developed a fondness for Moona, whom he had not previously met.

True to his word, in January Daniel began seeing fewer clients, retired from the law firm in late March and went into seclusion. In an effort to get his attention, she began dating another man in New Haven. The following February, she told him she intended to marry. The object had been to make him jealous. Initially, he seemed happy for her, until she told him whom the person was. His reaction made her feel trapped, rather than successful.

Maybe there was some truth in the words of a 'supposed friend' who told her: "You'll never marry anyone because you can't get loose from that fellow in Minnesota. He still has your heart." At the time, Emilia thought that Jerry was wrong, but when her fience drew a knife on her throat a week before they were to marry, she found herself positioned to marry another abuser. Laura, her neighbor and friend was totally against the marriage and begged her to contact Daniel for help. Bolstered by her friend's convictions, she called him.

"You'll go from the frying pan into the fire", he commented drily. "Of all the people that I know, you are the most marvelous person. Quit throwing yourself away on losers." She knew that he had given her good advice, but had he forgiven her for finding someone else? Would Daniel ever realize that he had her heart, not George? Her father, Alex Garland was also against the marriage. He talked to Arnie, and then told Emilia that she had to get out of the arrangement.

She had already purchased her new wedding dress, and dresses for Sheana and Moona her granddaughters, who would be in the wedding. Leah and Sheana, as well as Nicole and Moona had come from Minnesota for the wedding that was to take place in June of 1996. Nicole and Moona had moved in. Arnie expected them to find another place to stay before the wedding. His daughter and grandson had come up from Virginia as well.

All three grand-children were about eight years old, and Emilia had purchased special glasses for each of them. At the last moment, Alex called again and told her that he was in the hospital with a heart attack and needed her there immediately. There was an urgency in his voice that made Emilia cancel the wedding immediately and go to her father's side.

Leah and Sheana left before she did. Emilia was so upset at the idea of not marrying that she left New Haven for a while. She left her daughter and grand-daughter in the apartment with her dog, R.C. Her plans included attending a high school reunion in El Campo, Texas, giving a paper in Finland on epilepsy, then teaching in Lithuania before going to Australia to visit Bearta, her roommate from Yale. At that point she knew that she was in trouble with Daniel, and she knew that his advice was correct. Direct action was her only recourse to combat the depression which had set in.

Her father met her at the airport in Houston. He had helped her fool Arnie; get out of the upcoming marriage and away from New Haven. His health was fine he claimed. Alex drove her to El Campo for the reunion and picked her up two days later. Emilia looked up an old friend, and found to her relief that she had no interest in him at all. It was enjoyable to see some of her friends, and it would have been great to stay longer, but she left as the reunion was ending and flew on to Finland.

Everything in Finland went beautifully. It was Emilia's first trip there and she walked all over Helsinki. She even went aboard the submarine historical museum which was near her hotel. It was interesting to see how differently submarines were built in different countries. At the end of the conference, a group went to St. Petersburg, Russia on an outing. Emilia seized the opportunity to go through one of the major art museums in St. Petersburg, before heading for Lithuania. In Lithuania,

Emilia worked with other members of the APPLE Organization to teach special education teachers. She provided special education teachers with ways to better understand epilepsy in the classroom and teach art to special needs children. They wanted more information on both topics. Most of the people taught in universities in the States and donated time to the program to teach about their individual specialty. It was a unique experience as some of the classes required translators; others did not. While they were there, the group attended concerts, and visited various historic places in the country. They were housed in a dormitory setting which grew cold shortly before their two weeks concluded.

Later, it would be a relief to go to Australia and find spring, instead of fall. Emilia spent about six weeks on the sheep station of her friend Bearta Collins in Victoria. When they had roomed together at Yale in 1991, Bearta had invited Emilia to visit her in Australia. Bearta had an adorable little girl, Marguerite, who was 18 months old. Emilia was able to relax and forget her problems and just enjoy herself. While she was there, she found an article in a local newspaper about a 15 year-old girl who had just broken the record for the most money raised for the Spastic Society, as the Cerebral Palsy Foundation was known in Australia. She went to the near-by town and interviewed the family. While she was there, Yenta called her from the States in tears, as LaTianna, who was the same age as Marguerite, had been diagnosed with epilepsy. Yenta didn't know whom to believe. Emilia found herself counseling her daughter as she told her to contact the neurologist who knew the family for family history and to continue working with the hospital where her granddaughter was being seen. Emilia wrote an article about the Australian family and later gave it in Ljubljana, Slovenia at a conference on cerebral palsy. She had had to have the abstract written before December first, which was quickly approaching.

* * *

When Emilia returned home, she found that Nicole was going to school studying to be a Medical secretary and still dating the same young man that she had met earlier in the year. She seemed happy enough and was working at a local hotel as a housekeeper for a minimum wage of $7.50 while going to school. Moona was growing like a weed. Everything seemed to work for them. There was adequate space for Nicole, Moona, her dog, and Emilia in the apartment.

To her chagrin, she found that a mistake had been made in her credit card account and the account had not been paid. After clearing that matter up, she went to Boston for the American Epilepsy Society's annual meeting. It was her first visit to Boston. She made friends with several people who liked her art and suggested that she send in a picture for the Beth Israel Hospital's Neurological Calendar. She was among five American epileptics and six German epileptics who contributed to the calendar for 1997.

While in the Back Bay Mall in Boston, Emilia felt aware of someone tapping her shoulder. The young woman looked about her age and they began to talk spontaneously. Emilia realized that Reba was the daughter of the psychic she had visited while walking down Columbus Street the previous day. Natalia, Reba's mother had warned her about her feelings for Daniel, indicating that she would have to take care of him for a long time if she married him. The situation with Daniel had created a need to relieve the anxieties that it had wrought. These anxieties exacerbated her seizures. Natalia had actually cautioned her against marriage to this person. When Emilia and Reba began to talk, she was feeling extremely vexed, alone and unloved.

Emilia didn't recognize the fact that she had remained married for 23 years because she believed that divorce lowered her status. Love had never been a dependable part of marriage. As her parents had divorced when she was a child, she was certain that love didn't exist in marriage because people who loved her didn't marry her. Reba invited Emilia to come to her home and meet her family the next day. Reba introduced her to her children as well. Natalia told Emilia again that she shouldn't marry the man whom she loved because he would become extremely ill, and Emilia wouldn't be able to deal with it, or care for him. Emilia knew that Daniel's Parkinson's disease was something that had to be acknowledged. She would never forget how thin and frail his body felt in her arms when she hugged him. He had come over for lunch and enjoyed himself. He approved of the way that she had decorated the apartment. That had been an important day to her, as she valued his approval. Reba told her that she would be contacting her later.

The following month, Emilia went to Los Altos, California for another medical meeting and to find out more about genetics in epilepsy research. When she returned she had to acknowledge that her seizures were out of control as they were occurring every other day. She had lived with this most of the past year; but at this point, she talked to her neurologist. He suggested that she be seen at the Yale Epilepsy Center. It was March before that occurred and the manuscripts that she had been working on were nearing completion.

Section II:

March 1997-June 1998

Chapter II

Yale/1997

Emilia was taken off of one drug, gabapentin, cold turkey before she entered the hospital. Then her Klonopin was cut in half and changed to the generic clonazepam. Lemotragine was added. She wouldn't let them touch the Mebaral. It had prevented her from falling during seizures since November of 1994. At the center, she felt as if everyone was against her, everyone except Daniel. He called to wish her well, and tell her that he was going back to the South for more treatment for his Parkinson's disease. He was optimistic about having surgery. They agreed that medication changes were difficult to live with at times because of the side effects that drugs created. Emilia knew more about the side effects of lemotragine than some doctors did as she had brought a great deal of new literature back with her from Finland. The fact that it could cause cataracts was not mentioned by the doctor. Lemotragine was just being introduced to the United States, although it had been written about and used in Europe for several years. It had been discussed at length in Helsinki. Emilia felt as if people were not being honest with her.

Leah and her family had moved to New Haven in March to be with Emilia. On one occasion while visiting Emilia in the hospital, her three-year-old son, Simon pulled the bed handle so it went down too fast. At the same time, Leah told the nurse that her mother was about to have a seizure. When the nurse checked the EEG monitor, she was surprised that Leah was correct. Some of Emilia's seizures were subtle and difficult to recognize, but Leah had watched her mother have seizures since she was a child, and she knew that Emilia's eyes sometimes indicated a seizure was imminent.

When she returned home after the eight-day study, Emilia felt as though pots and pans constantly went off in her head. She was angry with everyone, and she knew that a side effect of reducing clonazepam too quickly was anger. The doctor had gone on a 6 month sabbatical and couldn't be reached. The secretary called to see how she was and if she had a rash. When Emilia demanded to speak with the doctor, the secretary grew angry and threatened to hang up.

"Don't you realize that one of the side effects of reducing clonazepam is anger? I need help. Now, either you call the doctor and tell her, or I will."

"I don't have to listen to a patient talk this way," the secretary answered.

"Doesn't she have someone who covers for her in her absence?"

"No. You say you don't have a rash; and you are angry because of the medication decrease. Is there anything else?"

"I feel as though I have lost part of my past." Emilia said.

"Maybe I should call the doctor. I'll call you back."

At that point, she realized that she couldn't deal with a neurologist who failed to have another doctor cover for her when she was gone. So she began looking for another doctor in the yellow pages. Before she found someone, the secretary called back saying that she would have to wait until the doctor returned to be seen, but to keep taking the generic clonazepam as directed. After Emilia hung up the phone, she found three doctors, whom she called. The only one who seemed even remotely dependable or interested was in Farmington, CT. She made an appointment with him for early May. Emilia found him to be a friend who would work with her until they found the right combination of drugs. At this point, neither the new doctor nor Emilia realized the extent of the side effects that the generic clonazepam would have on her a few years later.

Emilia was able to go off of lemotragine completely and reduce the Mebaral by 100 mg. But before that transpired, she faced a lot of problems.

The writing that she had been doing was affected by the new medications. Her slant on the book on epilepsy changed markedly. She felt the need to show how centers could misuse their patients. It seemed increasingly important to talk about epilepsy so that the physicians understood that consumers had feelings and that they understood more than doctors realized they did. Epilepsy had been with Emilia since she was two years old. It was no stranger. She continued working on the new version of *Epilepsy, a Personal Approach.*

Chapter III

Leah returns to New Haven

Leah, Eugen, and the three children stayed only two weeks with Emilia before finding a place to live. It wasn't the best, but it was home for them. Leah gave birth to her fifth child, Jeremiah in May. He was the only grandchild not born in Minnesota. He was long and thin and seemed quite healthy. Moona enjoyed having everyone over. That crowded Emilia's apartment, with four adults, five children and one dog. Eugen was concerned about his mother, who visited them shortly after she had remarried. He had trouble finding work in Connecticut because of his schizophrenia. Emilia understood the problem of working with a hidden disability. People had turned her away many times not because she was a bad person or incompetent, but because they were afraid of epilepsy. Of course, at the time she had felt as though she must be a bad person to have such difficulty in finding work. In July, Leah and Eugen moved back to Minnesota. In October, Jeremiah died unexpectedly and a stricken Emilia went to Minnesota to be with Leah and to find out what had happened. An autopsy was ordered and Leah and Eugen were told that their son had periventricular heterotopia. At the time, no one explained what it was. Emilia found that it was a disorder related to epilepsy that occurred in male children of women whose families had epilepsy, as well as a history of miscarriages. Three years earlier, they had confirmed that epilepsy was genetic, as Yenta, Leah's twin sister, had a daughter with epilepsy.

That Christmas, Daniel sent Emilia a Christmas card, the only one he ever sent her. Others had come for the entire family. It had three deer on the cover and a lovely verse inside. He had had the surgery for

Parkinson's in November, but it hadn't gone well. When she had invited him over for Thanksgiving, he had declined, saying that he needed to be with his brother's family. Emilia had wondered why, at the time. Emilia, Nicole and Moona had visited Daniel in August at his home. He hadn't looked that well then, and had difficulty talking to everyone except Moona, who kept him laughing.

* * *

In January, Emilia got a call from Leah, who was then in Arizona. The children were doing well in the new state. Simon and Arnold had asthma and the dry climate worked wonders for them. Sheana seemed to like the state also. Leah had been diagnosed with cervical cancer and was afraid that she might die from cancer as Emilia's mother had. Emilia waited until Leah had the surgery and then went to Tuscon. The AMA was having a medical meeting in Tucson and Emilia was attending, so she could use the travel as a business expense. On the way, she stopped in Houston to visit with her father, Alex Garland. He was eighty-eight that year, but as strong as an ox. He didn't tell her that his heart and blood pressure were bothering him; but she found out. He had sold his home in Sugarland, and moved to a retirement complex that offered assisted living near the Southwest Freeway. Alex didn't need the assisted living at that point, he believed, but it could prove helpful. Emilia had visited him two years earlier on her way to Finland and enjoyed herself immensely. Prior to that visit Emilia had not seen her Dad since Sheana was born in October of 1989. He had come to visit them in Minnesota and declared that he would never again fly north. He had no desire to be snow-bound.

Alex enjoyed Emilia's visit and made her promise to come again. He also admonished her for spending so much money on her children. "You'll stay broke if you keep it up, Emi. You know that. I shouldn't have to tell you something as elementary as that."

Emilia blushed, but said nothing. He was right. The fact that he spent money on her stepsister's son was not the issue here. The issue was Emilia's spending money. Better to say nothing and let it pass. When she arrived in Arizona, Leah met her with the children. Eugen wasn't living at home, Leah said. He had left them again. In truth, he was living there, hiding from her. Leah seemed upset. It was difficult to tell if she was using drugs again. If she were, that would explain why they never had money. If she weren't, then what was going on?

Emilia came in March, and she stayed with Leah until May. During the time that she was in their home, her ring was stolen, and she found herself dumped with the grandkids. Jeremiah's death had left an indelible scar on Eugen and Leah. He had seemed so perfect in every way. Two days before his death, they had married. Eugen loved Leah, but the voices that he heard because of the schizophrenia made life difficult for everyone. He shouted constantly in order to make them go away.

Leah decided that she wanted to go to Florida and be with Sheana's father to make sure that Eugen was indeed the right person with whom to spend her life. Emilia paid for their tickets and they flew to Pensacola, Florida. DW had found a house for them next to his mother's home. It had no window screens, poor plumbing, and about 33 more problems, but they lived there for most of the month of May. Eugen called continually, and Emilia disregarded the calls because Leah acted as though she didn't want to see him. Emilia began to wonder just whom she should believe.

The house was in such poor condition that Emilia called the city and they slapped a fine on their landlord. If he didn't correct the 37 problems that the city found, it would be boarded up.

Sheana had been in Florida when she was a baby, but she had no memory of her cousins. It was revealing to realize how much she resembled her father's family. Her grandmother, Mary brought over a fan for them that helped a lot. DW was a lost cause. He was there when they first arrived with his 'new' girl friend. Emilia realized that nothing about him had changed. He was still hooked on drugs and women. Sheana didn't want anything to do with him. Life in Florida was full of surprises. The neighbors dog trashed the garbage on a daily basis, the streets were supposed to be unsafe, but Emilia found an art supply shop that sold the Japanese water-colours that she liked to use, as well as an interesting art group. Unfortunately, she didn't have that much time to paint unless the kids were quiet.

She spent a lot of time walking by an old Jewish cemetery with beautiful flowers and gravestones. It was a perfect place to sit and sketch. She did this early in the day when Leah was at home. Leah worked at a fast food restaurant to make the money for the rent. She had constant migraines because of the heat, which came as no surprise to Emilia.

Emilia called Daniel once. She thought that he didn't call back until she saw the telephone bill and noted his number was on it. "I wonder why we didn't connect," she mused. Oh well, I'll be home on the 28th of May and I'll call him then. Emilia wanted to ask what she should do about the irresponsible landlord. However, she had managed by herself.

When DW's sister Gully brought her kids over, everyone enjoyed themselves. Mary came over and visited and Emilia taught art to all the children who wanted to paint. That was everyone except Arnold, who was only two and a half years old.

The next week, Emilia opened the back room, which wasn't used and found Eugen lying stark naked on the floor. She didn't recognize him and called the police. When they arrived, Sheana told them that he was their 'Daddy' and it was O.K. Emilia couldn't think of any way to refute her, so said nothing. When Leah came home from work and found him there, it was evident that she felt torn. She still loved him, but she didn't want to be with him.

They all moved to a hotel that was near Leah's work. It was air-conditioned. To anyone who has ever lived on the Gulf Coast without air-conditioning in late May, this is a necessity. Emilia flew back home on the 28th as planned, leaving Leah to work out her own problems with Eugen. As they drove by the house on the way to the airport, Emilia noticed that it was boarded up. Apparently, the city had taken it over.

Although Emilia didn't know it at the time, George had turned up at the house the day after they went to the hotel. He was surprised to find Eugen alone in the house and no sign of Emilia, Leah or the children. He bought Eugen lunch, but when he asked him for $10.00, he said "No" and left. The USS WALKER had had their annual reunion party in Pensacola that year. George would not give up the idea that he and Emilia should re-marry.

Chapter IV

Daniel Dies, Travel in Europe

When Emilia returned home, Moona and Nicole were glad to see her. Nicole was still working at the hotel, for she had been unable to find work as a medical secretary. The school had said that they would place her upon graduation, but five months had passed with no sign of a job. Emilia was relieved to be at home. In June, she was scheduled to fly to Ljubljana, Slovenia where she would give a paper on cerebral palsy at a Medical conference. The previous year, she had begun working as a beauty consultant with Mary Kay Cosmetics, Inc. She enjoyed her work, although she hadn't been as successful economically as she would have liked.

It took her a few days to recuperate from the trip. On the fourth of June, she called Daniel to see how he was. His brother, Ralph, told her that he had died on the first of June. His death was the result of a heart attack that neither the hospital nor the family had anticipated. Daniel was hospitalized because of a cold, and he had planned to leave the hospital the very day that he died. In fact that last evening, everyone had been in high spirits at his return.

Although her body felt frozen, Emilia felt as though she must be strong. She thanked Ralph for his kind words, hung up the phone, and began cleaning. It was good that she had to leave again soon, she realized. Right now, she didn't want to be alone, or with Nicole and Moona. She wanted to be with her friends. Milo, the paediatric neurologist holding the congress in Ljubljana was a good friend of hers and it would be a comfort to visit with him and his wife Tatjanna.

Emilia spent three days in Vienna at the pre-conference. She saw little of Vienna aside from the daily boat-rides from her hotel to San

Serverlo Island where the conference took place. Afterwards, she went on to Ljubljana for several more days and the major conference. Her luggage, which had been lost the day that she arrived in Venice, was still missing. Luckily, all of the slides and pictures that she needed she had carried with her onto the plane. While she was in Ljubljana, she met Dr. Wu, a paediatric neurologist from Beijing. As they talked, they realized that they knew several of the same professors at the University of Minnesota and had attended classes there at the same time.

"You must come to China in 2002, Emilia. We are hosting this same conference. Promise that you will try," she said persuasively. Emilia was delighted with the invitation and promised to get there if possible. It would take a bit of maneuvering, but she felt that she would go. While in Ljubljana, she bought two new blouses to manage as there seemed little likelihood that she would find her luggage.

The post-congress was held in Vienna. Emilia always enjoyed Vienna. People were friendly and always walked their dogs in the park. The day before she left, Delta Airlines finally delivered her luggage—eighteen days after she had left the States. After that, she went to Praha, CZZK Rep. to visit with Ivan Lesný, a neurologist who had been one of the four original people who set up the European Paediatric Neurological Congresses. He had always loved her work in words and pictures. This time, he invited her to visit his hospital—Motel Hospital. On her next visit, he assured her he would take her to the hospital in the mountains. Emilia found the hospital interesting. It was understaffed due to a low economy that prevented them from paying nurses as much as they would have liked. She watched with interest as one young girl had the exact Video EEG test done here by her grandmother, who was a nurse, which she had had in New Haven in 1997. Secretly, she believed that the grandmother, who was a nurse, probably recognized the seizures better than some of the nurses in the hospital in New Haven. Dr. Lesný was a person admired by his staff and friends. He had worked continuously as a neurologist during the Second World War and the innovations that he began had gone a long way to providing Praha with a leading medical centre.

Later, she spent some time at St. Charles University visiting with another doctor who worked with cerebral palsy. She was still dedicated to publishing the book that she had written about CP in the 1980's. It seemed necessary to learn new aspects of a disorder in order to present a clear picture of the topic. She returned to Connecticut somewhat hopeful that she would be able to rework the CP book.

In July, Emilia went to the Mary Kay Seminar in Dallas, Texas. Afterwards, she visited friends and family in central Texas and Houston. When she got to Mexia, she had a relaxing time on her cousin's ranch, before going on to Houston. That time, she didn't need to take a bus. One of her friends brought her to Mexia, and another friend took her back to Houston, where she spent some quality time with her father. She began to try to understand Alex. The more that they talked, the closer they grew.

When Emilia returned home, she kept herself as busy as possible. She worked on her art, writing, and Mary Kay sales. Still, she felt utterly alone. She no longer had someone who could make her laugh and allow her to retain the feelings of respect and understanding. Emilia realized how much Daniel had affected her life.

George was still around, but he had never treated her kindly or attempted to discuss anything with her. At that point, she had no desire to deal with him. She still hadn't been able to cry. It would be December before the tears would come and provide some release from the pain of Daniel's death.

Section III:

2000-2002

Chapter V

Problems in writing/painting in France

When Emilia left the Epilepsy Center at Yale, she felt that she had lost the ten years of counseling with Liza McDermott that had enabled her to see George for the abusive man that he was. She felt robbed of her counseling, yet knew that she must find someone else to talk to. Reba seemed to be the person best qualified for this. Emilia tried to recruit Reba as a Mary Kay Beauty Consultant, but she never really agreed to do this. By placing importance on Mary Kay, Emilia found an outlet for her emotions. Reba grew to be a good friend. She liked Emilia's art, and she bought some of the cosmetic products Emilia sold as well as her art. But her main assets were her love for Emilia and her ability to make Emilia laugh at herself.

* * *

When an invitation arrived in the summer of 2000 to take part in a watercolour class in France, Emilia jumped at the opportunity. She had never been to France, but she believed that it should be romantic. Emilia left two days before the program began and spent some time investigating Paris on her own. She went to Versailles, which lay outside of Paris, by bus and then returned to view Notre Dame Cathedral in the center of Paris as she sat by the river Seine. at dusk. Naturally, she found an art store near the hotel and purchased new colours and paper.

The members of the *Flying Colors* art class were to meet at a rail station near the hotel. Emilia got there early, but she had no idea what the people looked like, aside from the fact that they spoke English and were with *Flying Colors*. After two hours of waiting, she finally found the group and they set off for the interior part of France. First, they went to La Rochelle, then to Isle de France and later to the farm of one of their hosts. There were two teachers and ten students. Milford Zorn was in his early 90's, and his work was fantastic. Sheila Pearson was also a good watercolorist and their styles balanced one another well. Dr. Zorn was fascinated with the idea that Emilia wrote about epilepsy and cerebral palsy. He had an optical condition, myasthenia gravis that prevented him from seeing things as he used to. Yet, this didn't seem to impede his work. Dr. Zorn was known as a 'California style' artist. She learned that during the Second World War, he had worked with USA security drawing sketches that were needed by the military for various security operations. He once told Emilia that when they returned, she should take a course in drawing people.

One of the towns that they visited was underground. All of the homes and most of the stores were under ground. Only the graveyard was above ground. While they were talking, Emilia and another lady suddenly found themselves alone near the graveyard. Everyone else had disappeared. At last, they found someone else from the group and eventually arrived at the underground restaurant where they would wine and dine.

Most of the people in the group were Americans. Emilia realized that this was the first time that she had traveled in Europe and worked with 'just Americans.' At the medical congresses, there were people from every country. Emilia had always steered away from other Americans. She made friends easily, but she felt as though her art was more inferior to that of some other students. Emilia's work was the most abstract of the students. Most had been painting and showing their work for a long time, although there were a few who had never been abroad before. La Rochelle had a marvelous view of the water as well as the cliffs that jutted out into it. Everyone sketched and then painted. Emilia was still having trouble with proportions, so she spent a lot of time re-working her work.

She was fascinated by the churches, which they painted in Isle de France, the next town. Drawing a church wasn't as simple as it sounded. You needed to get the right perspective and proportions. Also, the shadows that fell across the building lengthened with the changing time affecting its appearance. Shadows did a lot to change the color and texture of subjects.

Everyone relaxed on the farm. They worked alone and together. Emilia found several cows brushing the flies off with their tails. She settled down to draw them. It was fun. She began to realize that art was really something that she could enjoy. She liked one drawing that Dr. Zorn had done of La Rochelle, France and asked if he would sell it to her. He did, and it hangs in her living room. She continued to correspond with both teachers when she returned home.

When she returned to the States, Emilia signed up for Drawing III, Life Drawing at Southern Connecticut State University. This began a journey into the world of art that would take her through a degree in Fine Arts and prepare her for either a master's degree in Art Therapy, Painting, or Psychology.

People wondered how she had managed to get into the Drawing III class, without taking the pre-requisites. She had simply stated that her professor wanted her to take Life Drawing. There had never been any question. Emilia had taken drawing classes in Minnesota, but not for credit. Most of the work she had done had been specifically Watercolour classes at Minneapolis College of Art and Design (MCAD) on Stephens Street in Minneapolis.

In the fall, she began the program of Fine Arts. It would take her three years to complete, but they were some of the best scholastic years of her life. Her seizures were under better control than ever before. She enjoyed what she was doing and she felt good about herself. She credited Reba with a part of this, for having a good friend was important. Jana was a fellow Mary Kay Consultant who enjoyed art, travel, and writing as much as Emilia. She proved to be an important friend as well.

Nicole and Moona continued to live with Emilia. There wasn't a question of their moving at that point. Emilia needed them there to watch the dog when she was gone and Nicole's income was too low to allow her to have her own place. Rent in New Haven wasn't low. They split the cost of the groceries and Nicole paid $140 for rent of the garage. The situation seemed to work positively for everyone.

*   *   *

In December 2001, Emilia went to the American Epilepsy Society meeting in Philadelphia. She managed to talk her teachers into excusing her for four days. Two days after she arrived, she received a phone call from Nicole. RC had died. Although he was 17 years old, Emilia hadn't expected it. He had been ill for several years though. Apparently, God had called him home. She left that day, cutting short the trip and returned to find the girls distraught. They had him cremated, and when she came back and paid for it, they sprinkled his ashes into one of the ponds that he used to enjoy walking near. It was closer to the house than the Atlantic and it was water. It seemed so lonely without an animal that they decided to get another dog. Emilia picked Pepper. Nicole and Moona wanted a Pekinese that untied everyone's shoes and had a shape bark. Emilia could see her attacking the Christmas tree.

Emilia figured that if she paid for the dog, she would get the one that she liked. Pepper was a Lassa Apse like RC. He even had papers. Emilia thought at first about breeding him. However, she decided that that would be more trouble than it was worth. As it was, he was larger than RC and it took a while before he adjusted to living in a condominium. The Lassa Apse was bred to protect, as they were once the guard dogs used by the King of Tibet. It had taken RC a long time to quit barking when the outside door closed. It took Pepper even longer. In 2004, he finally was forced to wear a 'no bark' dog collar that zapped him when he barked.

Chapter VI

Emilia continues at SCSU/Moona goes to Texas

Emilia's classes included Art History of Japan as well as drawing and painting. During the spring break, she took Moona with her to visit Alex. Moona's own father had never acknowledged her, and she hoped that Alex would be a good influence upon her. As it turned out, Emilia and Moona had a marvelous visit. Alex had been afraid that some of the 'younger people' who were in the 70's might not like her, as she was mixed.

"Does that bother you, Dad?" Emilia asked.

"Of course not, it's these 'younger people' that I'm concerned about."

Interestingly enough, Moona charmed her way into the hearts of many of the residents. Emilia's aunt and uncle in El Campo also met Moona. She was their great-niece. It was never clear after that whether or not they approved of her.

Because Moona was so short, Alex called her 'little bit'. She called him 'Big Daddy'. That seemed to satisfy both of them. He was well known for his poetic writing and recitations. People enjoyed his recitations a*t The Towers,* and he enjoyed giving them. After she had visited Alex, Moona began to write poetry.

The following spring, Emilia and Moona visited Alex again. They had an enjoyable visit. This time, they went over to El Campo and visited Malia's grave site, as Moona Wynelle had been named for her grandmother. They also shopped in El Campo for Nicole and Moona. Alex was 92, but he was still driving and Emilia felt safe riding with him. On the other hand, riding with George frightened her to death.

* * *

In the summer, Emilia went to summer school and took classes that she needed. She still had time to teach summer school in West Haven where she had worked for the past two years. Emilia enjoyed working with children. However, she was certain that she did not want to do it everyday all year long.

In September of 2002, Emilia packed for China. She had sent in her abstract, and was going to give a poster. She'd never been to China, but she'd seen pictures that George had taken there, and she had heard most of his stories of Hong Kong many times. Her great-aunt Alice had been to the Great Wall in 1930, and it seemed prophetic that she should also be going to Beijing and seeing the Great Wall in 2002. "Sister", as her family called her, had been a medical secretary, had had epilepsy that was mis-diagnosed, and had broken her hip early in life, as had Emilia. She had loved to travel, and gone around the world on $500 in 1930 woth her sister-in-law. When "Sister" died in the 1950's, she left all of her books and a trunk of treasures from around the world to Emilia, although she had many other great-nieces or nephews.

When Emilia arrived in Beijing, she found it a marvelous place. She had used chopsticks most of her life, and was completely at home with the food. In 2000 she had met another woman neurologist from Vietnam at the IASSID congress who would be at this same conference in Beijing. They had an opportunity to visit. She was in charge of the Asian International Congress that was a part of the larger neurological congresses. Emilia visited with Dr. Wu also. She made friends with several Chinese doctors who wanted more information about epilepsy sent to them. She befriended two medical students who liked her art. They were delighted when she gave them each a picture in thanks for their help in setting up her poster.

Before she left, Emilia visited the Great Wall, and the Summer Palace. The tour guide was convinced that she 'had Chinese blood coursing through her veins.' Emilia finally told her that her mother's family was part American Indian. "Oh, that explains it!" She said animatedly. "We were there first." Emilia smiled at her expression.

There were two veterinarians on the tour with her. One was from Canada and the other was from Italy. They talked about the differences that they had noticed in the country. One went to the deep interior of

China, finding it quite remote and different. The other remained near Beijing. Their conversation provided an interesting diversion.

On the last night, Emilia went out into the city and bought paints and brushes, and ate soup with the locals. She even got a hot pink sweater to match her black skirt.

On the return flight, she stopped again in Detroit where her bags were re-checked thoroughly. She learned that while she was in China, one of the inspectors had been caught stealing material from the bags and fired immediately. After 9/11, flying had become more difficult for everyone. The checkpoints certainly made life difficult for travelers who flew a lot.

Chapter VII

George begins to court Emilia

In June of 2002 George Blake arrived in town to beg Emilia to marry him—again. Although she wasn't over Daniel, and had no qualms about whether or not George could change, she was lonely. Emilia believed that Moona and Nicole needed their own space. Nicole was still going with the same young man, although she had turned him down in 1998 when he asked her to marry her. He seemed to have entrapped her much as George had entrapped Emilia. Nicole even complained that her boyfriend's demanding attitude reminded her of her father. Emilia avoided the subject of marriage as long as she could. One Sunday, they had gone on a church outing with friends and Emilia brought him to a lovely quiet nook in the woods. They sat and talked for hours and watched the sun going down over the water.

George didn't appear to be as intimidating as he once had. Suddenly, the idea of marrying him didn't seem all that bad. She accepted the ring that he gave her and began to believe that they could be happy. Simultaneously she feared that the old mannerisms of the first marriage would reassert themselves. Emilia desperately wanted a man who would respect her as a person. George had never treated her with respect before. Why should she believe that now was any different? Was God testing her again?

George had contracted Parkinson's disease in 1988, but he didn't show the trembling that Daniel had until 1992; but then Daniel had had it for twenty years when he died. It was only in the last few years, when he could no longer drive that he had sought seclusion.

"I can help you with your work, Emilia," George said proudly. "I can drive you everywhere you want to go. You have to depend on the bus or Nicole now, don't you?"

"Yes, but I manage."

"With me, life would be simpler."

As she looked at him, Emilia thought 'like Hell'. Aloud, she said "Maybe it would," as she drummed her fingers on the rocks. 'Emilia, you are sending him double messages again,' she told herself. This was a habit that was difficult to abandon. It had taken her ten years to realize that she had spent too much of her life telling people what she thought they wanted to hear, rather than what she actually meant. She could see this continuing into the future with George.

"Promise me you'll go to the Navy Reunion with me this year. It's in May, as it was last year."

"I can't promise you anything until I know my class schedules. It would be wrong for me to do that."

"Well, think about it."

"O.K., I will."

When they left the rocks, George had the feeling that there was nothing stopping their remarriage. He began to plan where they would marry and how.

Emilia, for her part was excited about being engaged, but she was afraid of marriage.

* * *

After returning from China Emilia went to Minnesota for a Mary Kay meeting with her Director's Unit. George took her to the meeting and they visited their daughter Yenta and her family. It was a long ride to Yenta's home, but it was an even longer ride to the meeting, which was on the other side of Minneapolis. Everyone seemed to be of the opinion that they were married, but Emilia began to become nervous about the situation. Her director was nervous also, as she believed that George would slow Emilia down, or sidetrack her as he had before. They had been neighbors when Emilia first moved to Minnesota in 1976—a long time ago.

That winter, Emilia felt like a pawn in George's hands as she read his letters about how they would marry at his Navy Reunion in

Fredricksburg, Texas. They could marry in the company of his friends. Their first marriage had taken place around his friends, rather than hers. Her mother was there, but only the friends she had made after coming to Hawaii were there. Most of the people there were George's friends, anyway. Emilia recognized the feeling of engulfment that began to sweep over her.

She talked at length with the minister from her church about the situation. The minister suggested that she write a letter, but in case she had second thoughts, she believed that she shouldn't send the ring back. Her ideas sounded reasonable enough to Emilia, and she agreed to write George. Her friends at school were surprised about her marriage to her ex-husband, for some of them knew of their history. The letter that she wrote stated:

November 13, 2002

Dear George:

The weather is beginning to get warmer. I hope that we don't have another ice storm. It has been unseasonably cold for this area.

The day that I talked to you, it was 19 degrees most of the day. It went up from 18. We didn't get any heat until 10:34, and the heat was off when I got up. A plumber will be here on Monday to check the pipes.

The mechanism that runs the furnace wore out and had to be replaced.

The service fee that I have with the Gas Company came in handy that night. Nicole is receiving your Nursing magazine.

I'm sorry that you felt it was necessary to remind Moona that she had to move. She is aware of that, and the way you said it gave her the impression that you didn't want her around. Children don't need kid gloves, but they do need to have people treat them with respect. So do adults.

I have been having second thoughts about the advisability of getting back together. I know that I said 'yes', and I consider you a friend

You give me the impression that you just want to move in here and relax.

I haven't had this apartment to myself since 1995. Before I have anyone else here, I want some time to get my own life together. I am having financial problems, trust problems, and a great deal of pressure is on me to make certain that simple things are done correctly. I need to straighten out these financial problems by myself.

I'm asking myself if you actually can show respect to another person and I are coming up with 'maybe he cannot.' Add to that my knowledge of the problems of Parkinson's disease and you can see that I have reason to question the feasibility of marrying you. It isn't a matter of loving or not loving the other person. It comes down to whether you can or will respect me. You didn't before; apparently, you don't understand your grandchildren's need for respect, so why should I believe that you will respect me?

The fact that we aren't around one another and I am not certain how things will work is putting a lot of pressure on me. I don't need that. I do not need to have three seizures a week again. I've been there and done that. I have also been doing great until the last seven months.

You can't decide that your health will not be affected by Parkinson's, or expect that health not to affect other people. I don't have the physical and emotional stamina to handle it. Neither do I have the physical and emotional stamina to handle emotional abuse. I have had a teacher this past semester who enjoyed making fun of the way that I asked questions. He succeeded in keeping me upset constantly. He pushed me, because he wanted me to learn.

One of my classmates and I both told him that he needed to be more kind when he pushed people to succeed. Does that sound familiar? It should.

He took a page out of your book of 'constructive criticism.'

I can't handle that from anyone, least of all from you. Life is too short to live it on the edge of your seat. I did that for many years. You haven't made me feel that it would be any different, although I am sure that you would try your utmost to change. You have changed. I am petrified of getting back into a similar situation. Sure, I am lonely at times. But I was lonely when I was married to you. The ability to enjoy conversation with another, not just existing with them is important to me.

I find myself saying things that I believe you want to hear. That is not right.

So, I believe that the best bet is to remain friends and live apart.

George, you have to listen to yourself. You are so excited about marrying me that you have forgotten to talk about what comes after the marriage. Sometimes things have been fine. Other times, we were both on edge and I can't see living that way. I feel badly that this isn't going to work out the way we had planned. Relationships are built upon friendship, and we just became friends three years ago. Friends could take it or leave it, and still work with one-another about the children.

After watching Daniel suffer with Parkinson's disease over a twenty- year period, I know for a fact that it can change your abilities in a split second. One day, everything is fine, the next like it or not, you need someone to take care of you. I do not think that I am that someone. There are too many emotions involved.

Sincerely,
Emilia

Emilia placed the letter in an envelope and mailed it to George. For a while, she didn't hear anything at all. Then she got a letter from him stating that he would be in New Haven at Christmas. Surprised, she wrote back and said it would be a good time to discuss her letter.

When George arrived at Christmas, Moona and Nicole were excited to see him. They hadn't had company for Christmas for a long time. Company was always welcome. This time, George brought a foldaway bed for himself. Emilia still wasn't allowing him to sleep with her, and he liked his own mattress. If truth were known, at the time, he was having difficulty containing his urine, and the less fuss he created, the better, he believed.

Emilia wasn't wearing her engagement ring when he arrived and he questioned her about this, acting very hurt and offended.

"I stopped wearing the ring when I wrote you in November," Emilia replied calmly.

"What letter? I never received any letter."

"I mailed it to you and told you that I couldn't handle you and Parkinson's disease emotionally or physically." She said a little louder than was necessary.

"Well, I never got the letter. Put that ring back on. We're engaged."

Emilia had no idea what to do. She didn't want to be engaged. But she put the ring back on to shut him up. During his stay, they took a bus once to the shopping mall. It was like *déjà vu* all over again. When they walked, they walked single file, George always in the lead. When they disagreed about anything, like whether to cross a street at one place or another, he insisted that his way was the *'only way'*. Emilia knew that she didn't want anything else to do with him after they had walked six blocks in December weather, crossed three busy intersections, and finally arrived at Wal-Mart to have only a cup of coffee that wasn't even good. By the time that he had left, she was worn out and glad to get rid of him. She still had a year and a half left before she would finish her bachelor's degree in Art, and Emilia wasn't about to concede that she needed him. But what should she do? If he never received the letter, was that her fault? Why did she need another guilt trip?

"He knows how to push my buttons," she said to herself. "I act like a nut case around him. The neurologist in Minnesota was right when he said that I couldn't live around him and maintain good seizure control. I'm not having as many seizures as I did then, but things are not as good as they were before he arrived."

* * *

After George left, Emilia went to Houston to visit Alex. She had promised him that she would paint him a picture in oils for Christmas. When she got there, it was after Christmas, but before his birthday which was January 2nd. For about ten or eleven days Emilia visited with her Dad and his friends at *the Towers*. She also spent some time with his friend Myrtle, as they were invited to her home for New Year's. Emilia could see that her Dad's body was slowing down. He was still taking a medley of medicines for high blood pressure and heart problems, as well as vitamins. He seemed more forgetful than he had on her last visit, and he didn't enjoy playing dominoes for long periods, as he usually did. Instead, he sat around and slept more and more. As he slept, his hands jiggled back and forth. The TV blared on, as his favorite newscaster gave the daily news. While he slept, Emilia sketched her father in different poses.

She had been pleasantly surprised that Alex liked the self-portrait that she gave him. She had tried her best. It was interesting that Alex had never asked for her watercolours, only for an oil painting. It said something to her. Alex still loved and admired her mother. Malia had done oil, watercolour and chalk; but her forte had been oil.

She had told her father about her trip to China. He reminded her that her great-aunt had visited the Great Wall in 1930. Emilia realized that now Alex spent more and more time talking about her mother and her family than he had in the past.

Two days before Emilia was to leave, Alex was rushed to the hospital. He had collapsed near the elevator, in what looked to Emilia like a mini-seizure. When she tried to explain what happened at the hospital, they paid her little mind, and called Myrtle, his lady friend. Myrtle was the person that the hospital contacted when anything happened to Alex. Neither Emilia nor her younger step-sister, Mae were contacted unless there was a dire emergency. Since Emilia was present, she felt that it was important that they know what had happened.

Myrtle took over as soon as she arrived. Emilia was told to leave in no uncertain terms. She returned to *the Towers* with another of Alex's friends who assured her that she had done the right thing by trying to talk to the nurses. That helped.

*　*　*

Later, Emilia went to Minnesota for a meeting honoring one of the women in her Unit who just became a Mary Kay National Sales Director. It was an interesting meeting, and Emilia learned a lot. She made new friends, and visited with others she had known for longer. George rented a room in the hotel in Saint Louis Park where the conference was being held. He continually complained about the cost, and whenever Emilia tried to start a different conversation, he changed it to something else.

She wore the engagement ring, but didn't like the setting. This month, she had begun working in oil, and the ring cut the canvas. The diamond was encased by four prongs that were as sharp as knives. The engagement ring that she had had before had been easier to wear. True, George had told her in 1987 that he had offered it to two other women before he offered it to her, but it had been compact and unique. This time, George wanted to start over with yellow gold instead of white gold, which Emilia didn't like. He believed that if he started with a clean slate, they could work things out.

Emilia brought her French books with her and got up early every morning to study them. She was trying desperately to get through the second year of French. She had had French in school from 1956-1958; but afterwards when she was in Europe she had reverted back to the Spanish that she had known since childhood. Languages were a challenge. If Emilia ever wanted to be able to speak French fluently, she had to learn French now. George considered her endeavors unnecessary. He was more interested in sex. Although Emilia had brought a lovely sexy gown, he froze and couldn't do anything when he had the opportunity. That suited her fine, because he always hurt her when he penetrated her fully.

"Don't worry, George. I don't require that much sexual contact. It is more important to me that you respect me for who I am." Emilia said casually.

"That's good. I still can't get an erection to stay up."

"You never could; why should that surprise you?" she bantered.

"I want you to be happy." George said lamely.

"As I said, sex is not the only thing involved in marriage. Respect is as important, if not more so."

Emilia was having a difficult time sleeping with George. She had never had sex with Daniel, but she had dreamed about it. In her dreams, they lay quietly on a soft bed beneath a railroad track, away from the world of reality; but the bed didn't shake at all. In contrast, every bed she lay upon with George shook like it was being run over by a ten-ton truck the entire time that they lay there. Emilia had difficulty separating her emotions. She seriously doubted whether or not she would ever be able to lie on the bed with George without thinking of Daniel, as he shook the mattress.

Parkinson's disease is a difficult disease for everyone in the family. It can change one's attitude and life drastically as an amorphous object that takes over your life and rearranges your emotions. Living with someone who has the disease is difficult, especially if the individual strives to maintain control and sees it slipping away. This creates a big problem for people who have always been in control, and never needed to depend on others. George denied the fact that his driving was unsafe, and continued to drive until his license was finally revoked in October of 2004. Emilia had never felt safe driving with George. Watching George's hands constantly leave the steering wheel because of the disease petrified her.

She prayed that God would watch over them, and he did. She had told her father on numerous occasions that she felt safer with him than with George. That made Alex happy, as Emilia was one of the few people who enjoyed riding with him.

When Emilia was among the other women at the meeting, she felt fine. But she noticed that noone came over to speak with her when she and George were eating alone. She felt as though she were on trial, but why? Was it because she was seeing a man who had abused her recklessly for 23 years? Emilia, who had wanted companionship and friendship from a significant other, also wanted friendship from the other consultants. She knew what it was like to be left alone, and she hadn't expected that to occur here. She felt rebuked by the other women.

It was a relief to leave Minnesota and return to Connecticut. Being with George consistently for five days had exhausted her. She enjoyed her classes, and passed her French by a hair. It seemed evident that her ability to speak French fluently would not occur unless she took two more classes, and that would take another year. Although fluency in French would be helpful in her travels and research, Emilia felt it was more important to conclude her degree in art as quickly as possible.

The summer of 2003, Emilia spent taking math courses in summer school. Her former employer had closed her business in West Haven and only had artists teach at specific places in a free-lance mode. In the fall, Emilia continued taking oil painting. This time, she drew *The Dream* and then painted it in watercolour and then in oil. Her teacher was impressed.

Emilia had hesitated about trying oil because it had been her mother's forte. She felt safer doing her work in watercolour. However, as the semester continued, she began to enjoy oil painting and to become more adept at applying the craft. Although her counselors had believed that she should be able to graduate in December, one last course in economics was still needed. She took this on Saturdays in the spring of 2004 and graduated in May.

Section IV:

April 2004-June 2004

Chapter VIII

*Alex dies/Moona,
Leah and Emilia go to Houston.*

In January, Emilia had called Alex and suggested that she come down for his birthday. He'd responded by saying "When you come, I always get too tired and wind up in the hospital." Emilia was a little surprised at his response, but that day, January 2, 2004, had been his ninety-fifth birthday. He hadn't sounded like himself at all. This worried her, but she agreed to wait and come later. The next month she called again and talked with him, he still sounded disoriented.

When the phone rang on March 8, 2004, Myrtle Roar, her father's lady-friend, began by telling her that he was in the hospital. Myrtle rarely called unless there was a problem with her father's health. She had called to tell her that they had sold his car in the fall, however. Tonight, they had spent the night in the emergency ward waiting to be seen, after Alex had been brought over from *the Towers*. When they finally got him a room, Myrtle had left. Alex had a history of heart problems, high blood pressure, and in 2002, he had broken his left hip when he'd had a light heart attack. Emilia was concerned, but Myrtle assured her that he seemed all right. Then she tried to make sure that Emilia knew what was happening. "If you get here next week that should be soon enough," Myrtle said and rang off.

Emilia called three airlines and arranged for two seats for the following Monday. After she made the reservations, she realized that she couldn't change them if she needed to go earlier. Moona would go with her. Emilia knew that if her father were ill, she would need Moona there. Myrtle was no friend of hers, and neither was her sister, Mae. She knew that she'd have seizures, and she needed Moona with her. Besides, Moona was already crying and begging to go.

Nicole and Moona had just rented an apartment in New London and were planning to move out later in the month. But they were still living with her. When he left at Christmas, George had made it clear to Nicole that when he came back; she had better be gone.

Later in the night, Myrtle called back. This time, the assurance that she had in her voice was gone. "Alex is in trouble, Emilia. After I left, they put him in a bed with side-rails. He woke up at two in the morning and tried to climb out of bed. He decided that he wanted to go home and had had enough of hospitals. He broke his hip again."

"Oh, my God," Emilia gasped.

"They can't operate because the anesthesia would kill him. I don't know what they'll do next." Myrtle said in a shaky voice. "When can you get down here?"

"I don't know. I have a mid-term on Saturday. I just made reservations for the following Monday."

"Well, I don't know how long he'll last."

"What do you mean?"

"Emilia, do what you can. But come down as soon as you can. He should be alright for a few more days."

"What are you saying? That he is dying?"

"No. Only that the doctor doesn't know what to do. She may have to use a Morphine pump. Bye."

Emilia hung up the phone and wondered just how ill her father was. She thought that she had done the right thing. She was trying to take the test before she left. Was that selfish, she wondered? What was a Morphine pump?

Next she called Rosa, a nurse from the Philippines, who lived in New York. She would know what Grace was talking about when she mentioned the Morphine Pump.

"Aloha Rosa, I need information. My Dad is really ill. What is a Morphine pump?" Emilia asked.

Rosa told her, "You must mean the 'Morphine Drip', which is used to allow people to die without excruciating pain. Once the Morphine Drip is started, Alex has about three to five days to live. It's used to give comfort to people who were dying. Emilia, I'm sorry your father is so ill. Call me back if you need to talk, but go as soon as possible."

"He is dying?" Emilia said in disbelief. After they finished their conversation, Emilia blamed herself for waiting so long to change the reservations. She felt guilty. But, she also felt angry.

The next morning she called another of Alex's friends at *the Towers*.

"Emilia, get here as soon as you can. Your Daddy isn't going to last very long. I called the hospital for him last night. It isn't good."

"What is the doctor's phone number, Ted? I'll call and talk to her."

"I'll give it to you. But I bet she won't talk to you. You know the privacy act gives Myrtle full authority. Here's the number though."

"I'll try."

"Get here as soon as you can."

Emilia called the doctor's office. As Ted had suggested, no one could give her any information.

About an hour later, Grace Gold called her. Grace was another of Alex's friends. She did his taxes, and Emilia remembered that last Christmas her dad hadn't signed the checks that he usually sent to her and the girls. Grace had signed them for him, and omitted Yenta completely. When she called her Dad back, he said that Grace was handling his finances now. He apologized for the fact that he had missed one of the children. "I just sign what she gives me, Doll." He said. Alex had called her that off and on for a while. Sometimes, he forgot and called her Mae. But most of the time, it was 'Doll' or 'Emi.'

"Well, looks like you better catch the next flight down here. They put your father on a morphine pump last night. Myrtle won't leave his side; she asked me to call and give you the information."

"I may have trouble changing my flight."

"My son is having trouble too."

"What do you mean? Why should this concern him?"

"He's one of the pall bearers."

"You mean they're planning the funeral?"

"Someone has to. He's dying, Emilia." Grace said caustically.

"Why wasn't I consulted?"

"You were. Myrtle has called you from the start of this. What's that Myrtle?" Grace said. "I've told her. Myrtle wants to know when you'll be here."

"I'll call you back with the information. And, Leah should be at Dad's Condo late tonight." Emilia added.

"Good."

Emilia heard the clunk of the receiver and knew that whatever she did, better be done fast. She called Leah and told her to get the next bus out of Austin for Houston. Then she called *the Towers* and told them to expect her daughter late that night. After that, she changed the reservations for Moona and herself; contacted a friend in Missouri City for help with transportation, and packed. Her school had already been contacted and the professor was aware of the family emergency. Nicole drove them to the airport early the next morning. The flight seemed to take forever, as there was a long layover in Cleveland. They flew into Bush International Airport in Houston, where they caught the usual bus to Houston, and transferred to the 'D' bus by the Greyhound station. The walk from Beechnut Ave. to *The Towers* seemed to take forever.

Moona tried to calm her grandmother. Leah had called the night before, saying that Alex had been dead when she got there. His body was missing, and no one at the hospital would tell her where it had been taken.

Leah was distraught when her mother arrived. The apartment was unlocked. Leah hadn't been given a key. All of the knickknacks and some of the furniture and paintings were gone, wiped clean. Emilia knew that certain furniture was to go to Grace; other things she assumed her sister had taken. The picture that was supposed to go to Leland Welch was gone.

"It looks like everyone got what they wanted." She said in as calm a voice as she could muster. "At least, they left the bed."

After Emilia and Moona took their bags up to Alex's apartment, they went out the back door and over to the hospital where Alex had been. No one would give them any information, stating that Myrtle Roar was the only person he considered family. They were told that as far as they knew, Alex had no children. The hospital cited the privacy act as their reason for not telling Emilia what had happened to her father.

When they returned to *the Towers*, she began to ask questions to see who had been in the apartment. The secretary told her that three people had been in the apartment the previous day. As Emilia's voice escalated in response, the director asked her to come into his office. Emilia was irate by that time.

"You know me and you know Moona," Emilia shouted. "We've been here before and I want to know where my father was taken."

"Why! He was taken to Smith's Funeral home. The wake is tonight. Didn't you know?"

"If I had known, would I have asked?" she replied sarcastically. "Where is Smith's Funeral Home?"

"I'll call Myrtle and find out. We have people from *The Towers* who will be going. Is there anything else that I can help you with?"

"Yes, I would like a key for the door, or the lock changed. It looks as though someone riffled through Dad's things already. I really don't want what I brought with me to be stolen."

"I'll change the lock immediately. I'll have to call Myrtle and inform her of that. She needs to be able to get in, but I don't want you thinking that anyone can get in." The manager was a heavyset man and he puffed a lot as he spoke. Emilia didn't consider him very responsible.

"Well, they can now!" Emilia said. "It's a little late for that."

He was as good as his word. A new lock was installed immediately on the door. Emilia was able to have a key that allowed her to feel assured that the things that she owned would be there when she came back. She was also told that after that night, they couldn't eat in the cafeteria.

Leah looked at Moona's shoes. "I guess maybe we should go shopping. We'll try to find you a black hat, Mom. But if I can't find the style you like, I won't get anything. Come on Moona, we need shoes for tonight." The two girls headed for the stores, and Emilia unpacked her clothes and hung them up. She hadn't heard from Myrtle since they arrived.

The phone rang, and the manager informed her that the wake was at 5:00 p.m. that evening. He added that if she needed a ride, she could go with Alex's friends in *The Towers'* van.

Hanging up the phone, Emilia dialed Rev. Apurro, her friend in Missouri City. He was glad that she had contacted him again, and apologized for not being able to pick her up at the airport. She had known his son, who had died from cancer, when she had played the piano for the Asian American Untied Church of Christ in New Haven. Ted and his son agreed to pick her up at 5:00 so that they could attend the wake. Emilia felt embarrassed about everything that had happened. Families were supposed to work together not against one-another.

She went into her father's office and began looking at the material in the desk. All of his address books were gone. Other things were filed haphazardly. It was evident that someone else had been looking for something. An American flag and a roll of stamps were still there. Pocketing the stamps, she continued to look through his material.

Leah and Moona returned with two pair of shoes, and new skirts that they could wear to the funeral. Emilia didn't expect to hear from Myrtle or Mae before the wake. It looked as though everyone was too busy to be concerned about her feelings.

At a quarter to five, they went down to wait for Rev. Ted Apurro. It was warm outside, so they sat in the shade and talked. He and his oldest son arrived shortly. Again, Emilia found herself apologizing for the need to call him. He smiled and said that he understood. She thought that she should invite him to the wake also, but she had no idea what kind of reception he would have from Myrtle and Mae who seemed to be running the show.

Once they were inside the funeral parlor, things flowed a little easier. She told the man in charge that she was Alex's oldest daughter. He in turn showed her to the viewing room. There were a lot of people there whom Emilia had never seen before. She tried to contain her anger and smile. When she saw Myrtle, it was evident that she was suffering from Alex's death. She was crying openly. Emilia and Leah went over and talked to her. Moona hung back for she had never met Myrtle. "Your Daddy was a special man. I'll miss him. He always called me at night and in the morning." She said. "Last week, he woke up at two in the morning and told me to get up. He'd dressed and made breakfast. I told him to go back to bed. It was the middle of the night. I think that he was much more ill than you ever realized."

Emilia felt the tears burning in her eyes. She had known something was wrong, but it looked as though her father had had other people looking after him. "I'm sure that you meant a lot to him," Emilia responded.

"I hope so. He sure meant a lot to me," she sobbed. "Let's try and make this wake as peaceful as possible. No hard feelings."

"Sounds good to me," Emilia answered. Then she walked over to the casket and looked at her father. He looked so pale. His hair looked all right, but his legs looked shorter than they should have.

"I think that they broke his legs to fit him into the casket," Moona whispered.

"Maybe; but something doesn't look right."

Later when she was in the rest room, Emilia turned towards a familiar face. "Emilia, it's been so long since I saw you. I'm your Aunt Edna, Alex's sister."

"I didn't recognize you," Emilia answered, as her aunt hugged her. "You'll have to meet my daughter Leah and grand-daughter Moona. Is anyone else here that I should know?"

"Oh you'll find a bunch of Garland cousins in there, and Mae and her family, of course. You did see Mae?"

"No, I didn't see her when I first came in. She could have been somewhere else."

"Let's go find those cousins. E.C.'s wife is here too. She's your aunt too."

"I wouldn't know her if I saw her," Emilia said. "I imagine the last time that I saw either of you was when Grandpa died."

"Were you there?"

"Sure, I came with Dad to the funeral. I was the only one who came with him." Emilia smiled.

Leaving the rest room, they sauntered back into the viewing room. Emilia felt a little more at ease. Later, she found Leland Welch, a friend from high-school days, and he offered to take her home. They were to meet at the same funeral home the following day, and from there go to the cemetery in Houston. Although there were other relatives there whom she knew, there were an awful lot of people and relatives that she didn't know at all. Leah and Moona thought that a lot of the people were friends of Myrtle and Alex's. At any rate, they seemed to have a little difficulty adjusting to the fact that Emilia's granddaughter was mixed. Moona was a beautiful girl, and everyone who knew her knew that she loved her great-grandpa. They just had the feeling that these people didn't approve. Emilia really didn't care. Leland and his wife took them home early. Everyone else was invited to dinner.

When they got home that night, they got food from the kitchen and cooked supper in the microwave. They used the three bowls that were left, and the cup that Emilia had brought with her. They found some paper plates as well as plastic knives and forks, but the silverware and dishes were gone. Emilia and Leah looked through the things that remained. There was a large square safe, but it was locked. They had been told that Alex's attorney would come by for the safe the following evening after the funeral. When they came by, Emilia got their address in case she might need to contact them.

The funeral wasn't much different from the wake. One of Emilia's cousins did pick them up, although he was almost late. Drake gave the talk about her Dad. Mae had introduced her to her birth mother and her aunt the day before. Emilia's only feelings were that her mother's handshake was limp. Dad had always valued a strong handshake in a person. Mae had found her birth mother the year after Francis, Emilia's stepmother had died. Alex had helped her find her, but he had resented the time that she spent with her. Mae's son Peter was only nine months younger than Moona, but he looked much younger. Moona was three inches taller than Emilia and looked older than thirteen.

Because Emilia wanted everything to go as calmly as possible, she said the least amount possible to Mae, and was as kind as possible to Myrtle. She knew that her father had considered her his soul mate, and she was grateful for all of the good times that they had shared. Drake gave her a picture of her father when he played football for El Campo High School. It had been Drake's mother, Aunt MaryAnna's picture. Drake and his present wife lived on a ranch in Mexico. They told Emilia that she was welcome to visit, but failed to give her the address. She rather doubted that she ever would. After the funeral, Leland offered to drive her back to *The Towers*. Everyone else was going out.

Leah and Moona decided that Emilia needed to go out too. So, they took the bus to a Bar-B-Q place nearby. It was late when they got home, but it was nice and warm, in comparison to the weather they would have faced in Connecticut. Leah left early the next morning before Myrtle or Mae arrived to clear out the apartment. Emilia told Mae that she wanted some of her father's things. She had marked them, but Mae would only give her a bookcase, two lamps, the picture in oil that she had done for him, her grandchildren's pictures, and the three plaques that their father had wanted her to have. She refused to give her the mirror that Moona wanted, or another lamp that Emilia had wanted. As it turned out, Emilia only got the plaques because she took a picture away from Mae and got in a shouting match with her. "Either you give me the plaques or I'll take this picture," she said with rancor in her voice.

"Give them to her, Mae," her husband said. "We don't need fighting. Where are they?"

"In the car, go get them."

"I'll stay right here with this picture until you come back," Emilia screamed.

"Don't be silly, we'll move it back to the apartment," Mae said.

"I'm not being silly. Why should I trust you? I will go back to the apartment, but that is all." She kept her hands on the picture until the trophies were in her hands. Myrtle led Mae out of the room and began talking to her at length. With the plaques safely stowed under her arm, Emilia and Moona went to another apartment and visited with one of Alex's bridge partners. Moona was afraid that Emilia would have a seizure, and she did have a little one. They were both in tears when they knocked on Mattie's door.

"What's wrong? Come in, come in," Mattie said. She realized that Emilia was having a hard time, and tried to console her.

"Nobody cares about Dad," Emilia said. "They just care about the things that he had. That's not right. I don't even know if he had a will."

Emilia and Moona returned to Alex's condo somewhat calmed down. They had been able to cry for Alex, without feeling that they would be made fun of. Most of the furniture and fixtures were gone. Emilia got the bed covers and a pillow, but the rest of the things in the apartment went with Mae and her group of movers. Mae's son Peter had come by with his father for a moment. Nobody wanted to talk to him. He lived with his Dad and stepmother in Katy, not with his mother.

After Mae and her group left, Emilia and Moona talked to Myrtle. She seemed to feel friendly towards Emilia. Emilia asked her what they were going to do with the clothes that were still in the closet.

"Jeb, one of the black men who works here, will take them all and sell them at the church bazaar. Your Dad wanted him to have the clothes."

"I talked with him yesterday. He's a friendly person. Someone can get some use from the clothes." Emilia said. "I guess we had better call a cab and go to a motel tonight. Our tickets are good for three more days. It may take me that long to rest up from this. It's been a difficult four days and I'm sure that you're tired too."

"Yes. I am. I'll miss Alex's calls. I won't miss him calling in the middle of the night though. I think that he suffered from dementia at the last," Myrtle said. As she spoke, she was folding Alex's shirts. "I'll take these four shirts with me for my son. He'll enjoy them. He thought highly of Alex."

Since there was no furniture left in the room, Emilia had been sitting on the living room floor, her back resting against the butler's pantry. She called a taxi on her cell phone after she had made a reservation at a motel near the airport. Today, they had too much to handle on the bus. Emilia was surprised that they had anything at all. She had taken four shirts and some other clothes that her grandsons could use when they grew older.

When they arrived at the motel, they were still far from the airport. They were close enough to a shopping center to Fed Ex some of the things back to Connecticut. Rev. Apurro helped them with this also. It seemed ironic that the only person who helped Emilia was a minister that she had introduced to her father, four years earlier. At that time, Alex and Emilia had driven out to his church and Alex had met his wife, Lee as well. They ran a day care for the Philippine families in the area, and one of the children, Nathan liked Alex, calling him 'Toto,' which means 'uncle' in Vassayan. From then on, the family had been their friends.

Soon after they got to the motel, Emilia ordered Chinese food. The Chinese food lasted them until they left. Emilia was very tired. She couldn't tolerate air-conditioning, so she wore one of her Father's shirts to bed every night. It warmed her and smelt of him. She called George that first night and told him about the funeral. She had thought that it might console her to talk to him, but was mistaken. He was just an impatient voice that criticized her. He wasn't Daniel. He never would be Daniel. George had never been able to console her when she was married to him; why should she believe that he could change? Emilia needed someone who cared about how she felt and was willing to let her talk and just listen. When she hung up the phone, she felt that the call had been a waste of her time and money. Later, Leah called to let her know that she had arrived home safely. That was a relief.

Emilia and Moona had two bags and one box between them. They checked all of the bags, and carried the box onto the plane. It needed to be carefully stowed in the cargo area on the second plane, but they got home with everything intact. Ever since *9/11*, less food was offered on airlines. It was a shame to pay so much and get so little, Emilia thought. Nicole met them at the airport in Hartford, and they were glad to get home. The entire week had been draining on everyone.

* * *

Before they left Houston, Emilia contacted the people who held Alex's trust and arranged for a copy of the trust and the will to be mailed to her in April. There had been no time or reason to talk to Myrtle or Mae about these, for they wouldn't have given them to her. But she was mentioned in the trust, as well as an unnamed child, referred to as 'dead'.

'Does dead mean dead, or 'dead-to-me'? Is my brother dead? Where is he or his heir?' Emilia asked herself. There is such detail in the trust about the 'issue' of the 'dead' child that it causes me to wonder if the child is actually dead. I remember Dad being gone a lot when I was eight. He only came home on weekends. He borrowed Grandmother's quilts to stay warm in the place he was renting. When I questioned Frances about those quilts, she denied any knowledge of them. That's the year that he and mother had their biggest fight that I remember, and it was about adopting a boy. If the child is mixed, that could explain why I'm so comfortable around mixed or black people. It might also explain why all of our grandchildren are mixed. Dad didn't put their pictures up until I brought them to him. Then, he did, although Myrtle didn't like it.' Emilia had logged in her journal on April 17, 2004.

Nobody seemed to catch this clause except Emilia and her attorney Patrick. They believed that another child existed who had died, or was considered dead. The bulk of the estate went to Peter, Mae's son by her first marriage. This was almost ironic, as he lived not with Mae, but with his father. When they had divorced, Alex had paid the alimony for a long time.

Emilia reasoned that her father had done this because he knew that she had some money of her own. But Emilia was determined to find out about the other child. She remembered the fight that her parents had had when she was eight years old all too well. Emilia could still remember Alex screaming at Malia that he wanted to adopt a son. That was the only time she could remember Alex screaming at her mother. It must have been important.

Alex's attorney hadn't thought anything about it. But the trustee at Merrill Lynch agreed that the language did sound as though there were another child. But who was it? Why was there mention of the 'issue' of the dead child? When she mentioned this to Reba, her friend agreed that there might be another sibling. She offered to help her locate him or her through her psychic powers. Emilia at that time believed Reba could.

Emilia had read enough legal documents to understand trusts. Daniel had told her once that the only vocation she shouldn't go into was law. He believed that she had too kind a heart to last in the practice of law.

After Emilia returned, she took the exam that she had missed and passed it. Before she left, she had been teaching art at the Jewish

Community Center, but after she returned, the class on cartooning was canceled. This worked for Emilia, because she had begun working on the book again. She had taken part of it with her to Houston and worked on it after the funeral. But for the most part, she had slept. Now, it was time to catch up. The book needed to be sent to the publisher in April. Every chance that they had, she or Jana worked on it.

By the end of the month, the book's editing was complete and it was sent to Xlibris Corporation for publication. Nicole and Moona were still living in New London, but Moona came every other day at 5:30 to wait for the school bus. Emilia really wasn't alone. Later she would miss these impromptu visits.

Chapter IX

May 2004

    Emilia knew that George would be in New Haven in May, and she secretly hoped that he would leave before her graduation. The last thing she needed was his presence there. Experience had taught her that he could ruin anything that she tried to do on her own to better herself. The only things that he couldn't affect were her painting and her writing. He knew a lot about woodworking, and enjoyed photography, but he couldn't paint. So, he couldn't tell her how to paint. He had tried to tell her how to use a computer. He had worked for a computer company since 1976, when he retired from the Navy. But he had fixed computers; he didn't run them.

    Sure enough, George arrived the week before final exams. He couldn't have picked a worse time. Emilia spent a lot of time at the University library avoiding him and studying. Once he took her to class, but that was a disaster, and he only tried once. The rest of the time, she took the bus as usual. Another time, he dropped her off with her Mary Kay products, as she had a vendor's table at the University's Student Center.

    George's Navy Reunion had been in Pittsburgh this year. He had a lot to show her and a lot to tell her. He suggested that they try living together before they married. That sounded reasonable enough, but Emilia knew that if he ever left his home in Minnesota, he would expect her to take him in whether or not they could stand one-another or not. He decided that he would set the date. They left it that way, and he returned to Minnesota a week before her graduation. That week was filled with exciting things that seniors did. It was exhilarating. Emilia even won a prize at a bingo party. They went into New York City and down to Chelsea Wharf. Emilia spent the better part of the day sketching boats and people. Later in the day, they had a party at the Wharf which was a lot of fun. She danced. Although she had no partner, a couple of people asked her to dance. Some of the people were young enough to be her children, but they were all there to have fun and enjoy themselves. Everyone seemed friendly. As usual, she pushed her new book, her Mary Kay products and her paintings.

In March, Emilia had arranged to show her art six months later at a local coffee shop in New Haven. She had had cards made to advertise her art show but she also used them to advertise the upcoming book. Life felt good. She felt young and alive.

On graduation day, Nicole dropped her off at the address they were given and she looked for the place to park near the Yale Bowl. She and Moona agreed to find Emilia somewhere in the stands after graduation. Inadvertently, she found the people who were receiving their Graduate degrees, as well as a professor that she was working with on another book. He seemed happy that she had found a second editor for that book, and wished her well. Although it was pouring rain, she eventually found the line that she needed to stand in and began her long walk to commencement. Emilia couldn't even remember her previous commencement at Texas Women's University. She had never been as excited as today when she would graduate from Southern Connecticut State University with a Bachelor of Arts in Fine Arts degree.

Unless one has had epilepsy all of one's life, it is difficult to understand how confident one can grow after having no falling seizures for nine years. Although the rain was coming down in torrents, it was a beautiful day. There were no problems to be concerned with today. Emilia was on the lowest dose of medicine that she had ever been given. This had affected her studies positively. She was attending SCSU, the only university in the area that provided assistance for people with epilepsy. That in itself was noteworthy. Emilia didn't use their assistance that much, but she felt that her teachers were more knowledgeable about the disorder than people she had known in the past.

The rain didn't let up and everyone was soaked by the time that the service was over. Emilia came down from quite high up in the stand to accept her diploma amid gales of rain and wind. Flipping her tassel to the other side to show that she had graduated and holding on to her cap with one hand and the diploma and her cane with the other, she made her way back up amid cheers.

For once in her life, Emilia felt the sweet taste of success. She wondered what she would do next. She had promised herself to take a year off and write, paint and sell Mary Kay Cosmetics and see if she could make her businesses grow. If she decided to go back in the fall of 2005, she would prefer to stay at SCSU, rather than change to Albertus Magnus, simply because she liked the campus and the teachers. It might be necessary to look for a different school, if she decided to get a Master's in fine arts. First, she had to take specific courses at Southern to get into Albertus Magnus' program on Art Therapy. That would let her have a chance to see if she could handle the psychology courses that they required. It would work, she reasoned. There were four options: English, Art Therapy, Public Health, or Fine Art. Because of the writing that she had already done, her interest was piqued by Public Health and learning more about genetics and epilepsy. Yet, she enjoyed art, and knew that that would relax her and allow her to have a career. She discounted the idea of teaching everyday at a school. She could see herself teaching during the day, but not every day. That was the reason that she hadn't gone into Art Education. Although it was a rainy day, it was a good day. Nicole and Moona were there and they were the ones who had stood behind her while she was getting her degree and growing stronger.

Chapter X

Graduation/ Trip to France/New book

There was another reason that Emilia wanted George to leave before graduation day. She was about ready to show her art in New Haven in June, and had sent one book to a publisher. It had been accepted and the galleys would be coming back in late June. She needed time to be alone with them and edit them. Emilia and her friend Jana had worked from January to April of 2004, editing and re-editing the material. She went through the manuscript, and then Jana proofread her editing. This way, they had been able to catch most of the major errors. At the last minute, Emilia had given it to a public relations person at Yale's Art History department to line edit. She gave it the finishing touches. Emilia knew from experience that George could wreck her concentration if he were around.

Before the galleys arrived in late June, Emilia would attend the IASSID Congress in Montpellier, France. She would be giving a presentation on 'Depression and Epilepsy.' Nicole and Moona moved back into the apartment while Emilia was in France. Then Moona went to Texas to visit her Auntie Leah and left Nicole and Pepper alone. Nicole was relieved when her mother finally returned.

The galleys were sent back in late June, after Emilia had returned from Montpellier, France. She had had a rough trip in France, although the conference was very useful. The change in the price of the euro and the dollar created a problem for any person using American currency. The Euro was worth $1.68, changing the value of a $20.00 traveler's check to only $15.00. She had had to ask George to help 'bail her out' when her purse was picked and her identification and money were taken. That had made him happy, but not Emilia.

She took some lovely pictures in the mountains that she later used to sketch. There were interesting pictures of Devil's Bridge, and several churches in the mountains. Two days before she was to leave, she fell on her back while photographing a new area of Montpellier. She picked herself up from the unforgiving cement and kept walking. It became difficult to go far without stopping to rest. She sat down, rested and sketched. There were two drunks lying in a flower bush near the center of a fountain which was located on the center of town. She avoided them, but found a place to sketch the flowers. Later, she did the sketch in watercolour. She also found a palm tree that she liked, as well as some fixtures on houses that were intriguing to sketch. When she'd been in France in 2000, her art instructor had impressed upon her the importance of sketching as opposed to merely photographing material. She'd learned to keep a sketch-pad near by.

The next day she had trouble moving her back. She soaked in the shower; afraid to lie down in the tub for fear she couldn't get out. So, she propped up her back, placed her legs up on the chair, sketched and painted for two days. When she finally got ready to leave, she hadn't eaten anything but raisins and kiwis for three days. But they worked.

When she left, the hotel concierge told her she only needed thirteen Euros to get to the airport. He was wrong and when the taxi driver realized that she didn't have the twenty Euros that he wanted, he threw her luggage, and then her into the back of his taxi while he went off shouting for the Gendarme. Emilia picked herself up, and headed into the airport. She left the change on top of his car. The five Euro pieces he had already absconded from her. He refused a traveler's check, and he refused coins. It was evident to Emilia that President Bush's foreign policy had made no friends in France. In contrast to the pleasant visit she had had in 2000, France and French people wanted only money from Americans. She wondered what would ever bring her back to the country that Daniel had loved. She still had not seen the Louvre.

When she returned, she had to see a doctor about her back and her stomach, which hurt because of the pain pills that had been prescribed. All in all, Emilia spent ten days recuperating from her trip. Her topic had been 'Depression and Epilepsy,' rather appropriate for the session that she had in France.

Emilia prayed that she would finish editing the galleys, and begin the major work on the second book before George arrived on July 18, 2004. Mercifully, her prayers were granted. He was a day late, and the book was in press after the one editing of the galleys that Jana, Emilia and Maria did. Maria cautioned them that there should be more line editing, but at that point, Emilia and Jana realized just how much 'carving' they had done. It would have to be enough.

Jana and Emilia were excited about the new book. Emilia had used a copy of one of her oil paintings as the cover design for the book. It lowered the publication price considerably. Xlibris is a demand publisher and publishes books as they are ordered on demand. The author receives a certain percent of the royalties, and retains all of the rights. *The Spider's Net, a Family's Struggle with Abuse and Epilepsy* became available September 20, 2004 on the Internet, as well as in bookstores.

The other book that Emilia was re-editing had been thoroughly reviewed by a young woman at Yale, whose specialty was epilepsy. She did a wonderful job of analyzing which changes had to be done. Emilia was faced with a lot of editing that she hadn't anticipated. It went quickly, though. She completed it in August, after George had arrived. It was a relief to send the book to the publisher.

Section V:

July19 2004-October 1, 2004

Chapter XI

Bumming around on Emilia's Turf

"I'm here, honey," George said as she opened the door in mid July. "Just give me a little corner and I won't be in your way at all." He was only carrying a small bag in his hands, as if he were only planning to stay for a short time. George took Emilia in his arms and planted a slobber filled kiss on her lips. The Parkinson's made his mouth and nose leak constantly.

"I thought that you were going to be here yesterday," she said, instinctively backing away from him. She hadn't remembered his drainage as being that bad.

"Well, I got as far as Philadelphia, and the police stopped me. They said that I looked as though I didn't feel too well. They made me go to the hospital; then go to a motel, which they picked out. Then they took my car, returning it in the morning. I had to wait until today to get it back."

"They probably were trying to prevent an accident."

"I don't know why. But it was just as well. It was raining a lot and I had trouble holding the car on the road. I needed to rest, I just didn't want to."

"Well, now you're here safely. That's the main thing." Emilia said. "Did you bring your folding bed?"

"Oh, I left that in Minnesota. You have a bed. That's all we need."

"I suppose you're right," Emilia replied, questioning whether or not she would be able to sleep with him. "You suggested living together before we marry. That's a good idea."

"Well, it might give us an opportunity to get used to one another all over again." George said, smiling. "It's so good to see you, Emilia. Now that I'm retired, I want to live the life of a bum."

About that time, Emilia heard Moona coming in the kitchen door. "Guess who's in the living room, Moona?"

"Grandpa?"

"Yes. He just arrived." Emilia said and then hastened to explain. "Nicole and Moona moved back to New Haven. The apartment that they had was sold, and they are waiting until August first to get a new place in New Haven. It'll be nice to have them nearer."

"I hadn't expected that. But it's O.K." George said sullenly.

Emilia looked at him as he sat on the couch. He shook constantly. He had been a tall thin man. Now his back was bent over and he had difficulty standing and sitting straight. His hands and arms moved constantly. She noticed that he didn't stay seated very long either. He was constantly getting up and moving.

"I'm going out to the car and bring in the bags," he said. "Do you want to help me, Moona?"

"Not really, but I will." Moona replied as she stood up. There were four large boxes and two large suitcases. The suitcases had rollers on them, but the boxes had to be carried carefully.

George brought the boxes in one at a time. The warm weather caused him to sweat profusely. Emilia was glad that Moona was there to help. He stacked them by the front door, in front of the marble-topped table that had belonged to Emilia's great-grandmother, blocking the piano.

Emilia suggested that George put one of the suitcases in the bedroom, on the far side of the room where he would be sleeping. He also had a plastic box that he put in the bedroom where he stored his clothes.

"You can put your clothes in these four drawers," Emilia had said, indicating the drawers near his bag.

"OK. What's for supper?" George asked, making no move to use the drawers. "I'd like to take you out, if you don't have any objections."

"That would be lovely. Nicole won't be here until late tonight, so we might as well go about five." Emilia replied.

"It's almost five now. Let's go to *Friendly's*?" George said. "It's the day after your birthday, and we could celebrate it."

"You like their ice-cream Sundaes." Emilia said.

"So do I," Moona added.

"Let me change clothes and brush my hair. I must look a mess," Emilia said. "Then we can go."

"You look fine the way you are," George said. "I'd like to take a little nap, though. I'll just rest here on the couch for an hour."

So saying, he put his head on the throw pillow and was out like a light. The trembling didn't stop when he slept and Emilia worried that it would always be with him. She could imagine that Daniel had been this way the last year of his life. He had remained apart from her that last year, only seeing her once when they visited him 10 months before he died. She would never forget how he had shaken, and how distraught he had looked that day. He looked uneasy because they had come without calling first, and it had been Moona who had kept the conversation going, not Emilia or Nicole. He was so thin, and he had shaken so much that Emilia had had difficulty realizing that it was the person who had been there for her over the last 39 years. Now, she saw George's actions as reflections of Daniel's, Emilia knew that a meaningful relationship with him would be difficult. Still, she had to try in all fairness to him. Reba had insisted that it would work.

* * *

At 5:45 p.m., she woke George and the three of them went to *Friendly's* for supper. It was a treat for Moona and Emilia, who rarely ate out. Usually, Nicole and Moona wanted fast food. None of them had money to spend on restaurant fare. When they left *Friendly's*, everyone had something to bring home. George was surprised that even he couldn't eat everything and still have room for desert. He insisted that they sing "Happy Birthday" to Emilia. Everyone dug into the sundae. It was a huge ice-cream dish filled with ice cream, whipped cream, and topped by a cherry and chocolate sauce. Emilia could see the pounds coming on as she ate. The restaurant was air-conditioned, and the ice cream made her colder. Invariably she forgot to bring a sweater when she and George went out in the summer. This had resulted in pneumonia on more than one occasion. She believed that the sundae would have tasted much better outside if a cool breeze had been blowing. But, she wasn't buying, so she smiled and made light conversation. She watched as George struggled to hold his silverware. Parkinson's disease was taking a toll on him. When they left, Emilia and Moona buckled up quickly. George drove back home with difficulty. It was growing dark, and it was evident that he had trouble seeing late at night. When they got to their street, he went over the curb as he turned. Emilia had noticed over the past year that he did this a lot. When he was there in May, he had hit bushes, run lights, and skidded too close to the curb more often than not.

"I'll need to get a Connecticut drivers' license next," George commented. "If I am going to live here with you, I need to get it soon."

"Nicole can show you where to go. It's a bit of a drive from here, and I only know the bus route," Emilia replied.

As they got out of the car and went into the house, Moona carried George's food and her own. Emilia carried her own. Moona opened the door for them and held it while everyone filed through. When they got inside, Pepper was excited by the smells from the food, and Emilia wondered whether he was glad to see them or just the food. His 'No-Bark' collar wasn't working. George took it off of Pepper, tested the batteries with his battery charger, and then replaced the battery that was in the collar. "Now, it should work." He said, satisfied with himself. "Why does he have to wear this?"

"Because, the condominium association doesn't want barking dogs," Emilia said.

"I heard another dog barking. What about him?"

"He gets away with murder. That dog bit RC and caused him to have a nervous condition. His owner, a physician of all things, never did offer to help me pay for the veterinarian's bills he created. He said it wasn't his fault."

"Why not?" George asked.

"When it happened, his roommate had been walking their two dogs. The room-mate dropped the leashes. So, technically, I suppose Leo was not to blame, but his dog sure was."

Nicole came in minutes after he had adjusted the collar. She was glad to see her Dad, and hugged him enthusiastically. Everyone was tired, so Nicole and Moona pulled out the couch that turned into a bed, and made it up. George and Emilia told the girls 'good-night' and went to bed, Emilia insisted on a shower before bed, and George tried to join her in the shower. It was a fiasco, because he couldn't stop shaking long enough to stand still. Still, they managed. Emilia was glad that she knew what to expect from him, but she really worried that he would want sex tonight. He had always hurt her when he penetrated. Tonight things didn't go as George wanted. He couldn't stop shaking. "I think

I'm getting too old for this type of thing." He said. "I hope you don't mind."

"You're tired, George. We can wait," Emilia answered. Turning over, she tried to sleep. The bed shook continually. Although George was asleep, the trembling continued. Finally, about two in the morning, he got up.

"I can't sleep anymore." He said.

"What are you going to do?"

"I need to walk. I'll walk in the kitchen. Better yet, I'll take Pepper for a walk."

"Don't forget to take the key."

"Where is it?"

"The key is on the kitchen counter." Emilia answered.

George was up and dressed. When he got to the kitchen, Pepper was ready to walk. They took the key with them and went out for a turn around the block. Pepper was excited to go walking at night. George had taken him out before during his visit in May, but never this early in the morning.

When Emilia got up, George was reading the paper, and Pepper was lying at his feet. The girls were still asleep in the living room. George had made coffee in his cup, and had a bowl of cereal, as well as a piece of toast and peanut butter. Emilia slept after he got up. Before that, she hadn't had a wink of sleep. It looked as though living with George would be a real challenge to her sanity.

Maybe, if he got up during the night and left the bed, she would have a chance to sleep. Emilia was relieved that he hadn't pressured her into sex. He'd given up, when he realized he couldn't hold an erection. Moona slept most of the morning. Nicole got up at eight and had breakfast.

"When are you going to get your new apartment?"

"July 31st, I'm sorry that we have to crash here for a while, Dad, but there's no other way." Nicole said.

"Tell me again what happened to your apartment in New London? It seemed nice, when we visited there in May."

"Oh, the owner sold it to another person. She had to return to Puerto Rico because her father was ill. The people who bought it first told me that they would rent it, then, last week they decided not to rent. So, we are without a place until the new apartment is ready." Nicole explained. "I'll miss the apartment in New London, but I won't miss the gas prices it took to drive there and back. This place is only five minutes from here, and ten minutes from my job. Moona is close to school, and she will only be over here when I have to go to work early. Otherwise, she'll be fine at home."

"That sounds good," Emilia said.

"So you'll be here for eleven more days," George said.

"That's about right." Nicole replied. She began to feel as though her father was railroading her out of her mother's home. She wondered why her mother was considering re-marrying him. She had changed a lot since she'd been in Connecticut. She was much stronger than she had been. Nicole worried that everything would reverse itself, and somehow, her father would make her mother's life a living hell.

"Your mother says you can show me where the Motor Vehicle Department is. Can we do that today?" George said.

"I guess so. But I don't know if they are open today."

"If you show me, I'll be able to get there by myself."

"O.K," Nicole said. "Want to go now?"

"Sure. I'll follow you."

"No. I'll drive you over there. If you have to wait, I can come back for you."

After Nicole and George had left, Emilia had another cup of coffee. She was tempted to lie back down in bed. But she knew that she should be doing something else. She tried to envision how George expected to get a driver's license. Anyone who watched him drive would question his ability to focus and keep his hands on the wheel. Riding with George was like riding in a death trap. It always had been, in one way or another. She could still feel the bounce the car had taken in May, when George had hit a parked car and practically torn his right mirror off. It had been a dark street, and George couldn't see what he was doing, plus he kept allowing the wheel to go to the right. It was as though he couldn't keep focused on what he was doing. "It would be better if they refused him his license," she said aloud. "But then there would be no living with him. I can't imagine George riding a bus."

Chapter XII

Emilia works

Emilia went on working on the second book. She wanted it done by the end of August. To do this, she asked George to take the dog out early in the morning, and she slept late. Then, after breakfast, she would work. At 11:30 George would come in and announce that it was lunchtime. Some days, she stopped typing and fixed lunch, other days, she told him to do it himself. She wasn't that hungry. Somehow, mercifully she got through the manuscript, and sent it off to the New York publisher. (This book, *Epilepsy, A Personal Approach, 2nd Ed.* was edited by Dr. Nwangwu and Emilia.)

George wasn't as much help as he had said he would be. He needed to be looked after like a child. Emilia soon found that he would occupy all of her time if she let him. After the book was gone, George suggested that she should put hanging files in all of her filing cabinets.

"When I worked for Control Data one thing I did was file things. I want to help you become more efficient."

"Don't you think that I'm efficient?"

"You could be better. Do you know exactly where everything that you have filed is?"

"Well, no. And there is a lot of material that needs to be filed."

"See. I can help you. We'll go to the store and buy new hanging files for all of you filing cabinets. I'll install them personally."

Emilia wasn't sure who was going to pay for these files, but it sounded as if George were. She knew that it would take a long time, and she had wanted to start work on the book on Cerebral Palsy in September. Still, he did have a point. And she did need to find out where some of the material on cerebral palsy was. It would occupy him doing something that he liked. So, she agreed to go along with his plan.

It didn't take long for Emilia to realize that he had difficulty working with his hands. But George didn't give up. He kept working on his project. They had to make several trips to the store, and they both paid for the files. There were times when Emilia feared for the lives of her metal filing cabinets. However, he managed to put the files and their holders into all of the cabinets. After he had finished, she had to go through all twelve of the drawers individually and re-file everything. This took almost a month.

The subject of marriage had been pushed away, as the minister was out of town on vacation, and convention required six weeks of counseling before marriage in the Episcopal Church. When they finally did meet with Bary, the priest, they were angry with one another about several things, including the files. "Maybe you should live together in sin, like my parents do. It's more economical that way, "Bary joked. "No, seriously, you've been living apart for quite a while now. It may take a bit before you are ready to live together as one. Let's meet again in a month and see how things have progressed. That would be September 28th. OK?"

"Sounds good to me," Emilia said.

"Yeah, OK. By then we should be ready." George replied.

"So, we'll meet again September 28th. If there is a problem, let me know." Bary said.

As they left, George looked pleased and perplexed. "I thought that things would be much simpler than this. I didn't realize that the church would make us wait and get counseling. Where did you meet Bary?"

"Don't you remember? When mother was so ill in a nursing home, Nicole and I came to New Haven to find a priest to visit her. He was our choice. We've known him since 1979. That's a while, I would say."

"Oh."

George couldn't contain the irritation that crept over him as he tried to keep his hands from trembling. Nothing seemed to work. They had taken the bus today, so that he wouldn't have to pay for parking. Secretly, he was glad that he wasn't driving.

"Why don't we stop at *Claire's* and have something to eat?" Emilia suggested. "I remember that you used to like to have coffee in the mid-afternoon."

"I could go for some food, but no coffee. I can't drink it after four o'clock. It keeps me up at night."

"They have tea also, as well as good food." She promised.

"How far is it?"

"Directly across the Green; shall we go?"

"OK."

"Remember what Bary told you about conversation? He suggested that you should talk to me more, if you wanted me to marry you. He's correct. You've never been one for talking anymore than need be, he can be forgiven for not knowing that."

"You talk enough for both of us."

"That's not the point. I can't think your thoughts or read your mind." Emilia turned, facing George. His back was humped, and the fluid was flowing out of his nose and his mouth. It seemed to get worse in the heat. This was late August, and it was hot. Emilia wondered whether the nasal drip and salivation could be stopped, and if not, whether she could live with a man who constantly slobbered all over himself.

When they reached *Claire's,* Emilia ordered coffee and a mini loaf. George decided to have the same. Mrs. Beasley, the owner came over and visited with them. Emilia planned to show her art there in October, and now she was talking about the possibility of a book signing. Emilia had just received the author's copy of her new book that would be available on the Internet in late September. While they talked about when to have the book signing, Mrs. Beasley asked George if he liked Connecticut.

"Oh, yes. I haven't lived here in New Haven before; but we lived in New London for two years. I enjoyed that. It's nice to be near the ocean."

"Yes, it is. At one point, this part of the city was closer to the ocean than it is now. This is known as the coldest corner in the city because of that, some say." Mrs. Beasley commented.

"Not to change the subject, but how many pictures can Emilia hang here?" George said.

Turning to Emilia, Mrs. Beasley asked, "How many did you hang last time?"

"I think I hung about sixteen." Emilia replied. "But then, I hung pictures over to the left of us, and I don't see that available to me."

"That sounds about right."

"I have a cart that she can carry all of her pictures in," George said.

"Good." Mrs. Beasley said. Noticing, George's trembling hands, she stood up and added, "I have to go now and talk to some other people. Talk to you later."

"She seems nice."

"Yes."

"We better leave pretty soon. Where do we catch the bus?"

"Two blocks down."

George got up and walked out. Emilia followed him. He never walked with her, always in front of her. She wondered when George's finances would be transferred from Minnesota to Connecticut. He had insisted that his bank was at fault, but Emilia was uncertain. He had come in mid-July, with only a set amount of money to spend. He contended that it would be late September before he would have his money transferred. She had no idea what he expected her to do. Support him?

Chapter XIII

Labor Day

On Labor Day, Emilia and George were invited to Hamden for a cook out. One of Emilia's friends, Judy invited them to meet her at another friend's house. George and Emilia had the directions, but they got lost. As always, George refused to ask for help until he had driven for thirty unneeded minutes. Although she knew they were lost, Emilia tried to enjoy the drive. It wasn't as hot, and of course, George's car had air-conditioning and the scenery was different. She hadn't been to this part of Hamden lately. It was wooded and green. When they got there, she relaxed. Eventually, Judy arrived. Their hosts liked art and writing, so Emilia found herself among friends.

Before she left, she had the name and address of another artist, as well as the location of an art gallery in New Haven that she hadn't tried. On the way back, Emilia could see just how thin George was. He had worn suspenders today, and it was all too evident that he was underweight. She thought that the disease would not give them much time together. In spite of herself, Emilia believed that she was falling for George again. She'd tried not to, but she had been lonely without a man around. She told herself that he had mellowed out and was more congenial. Her emotions kept blinding her to reality. Although she knew that her seizures had increased, she didn't put the full blame on George. She had to ask herself if she liked being angry so much. The answer was no, but what could she do? Emilia felt sorry for the man. It was easy for her to 'care take' George. This time, he couldn't do much to argue with her. The reality of the interference that he would create in her life hadn't dawned upon her.

George seemed impressed with the people that he had met. They seemed to have enjoyed some of his favorite stories. As an ex Navy man, George loved to tell stories of all types. He especially enjoyed telling stories that put Emilia down. He gloated over the fact that he had been able to successfully place all of the hanging file holders into the filing cabinets. As they were leaving, the sun was going down and George grew a little anxious about his driving. They drove home without incident until they reached the last corner. There, George's car went over the corner, which had only a modest curb cut, and bounced senselessly into their street. When he got to the apartment building, he decided to park in front, rather than put the car in the garage.

Emilia bit her tongue to keep from saying anything negative to him. She didn't want to spoil what had been an enjoyable day. By the time that they returned home, the block party that was held annually in the street was over. Just as well, she thought. He might have hit someone. It had been pleasant to have a date tonight, but she had to really examine whether she wanted George around 'always', as his favorite song implied.

When they returned home, Emilia made some tea. The hot weather had made her feel dehydrated, although she had drunk several soft drinks at the party. Her Dad had always told her that a hot cup of tea or coffee would cool her off. George joined her. They sat at the table, watching the dog lounge on the floor. "I'll take Pepper out when I get rested," he said. The next minute, he was nodding off to sleep.

Emilia finished her tea, found the key and took the dog for his walk after she had been fed. When she returned, George had moved to the couch and was sound asleep. His body was in a contorted position, as his head hung forward and his saliva and nasal drip dampened his clothes and the couch. His hands were folded and his legs were in a seated position. She debated whether to wake him or not. Finally, she decided to let him sleep.

It had been a long day, and she knew that if he went to bed, he wouldn't sleep.

"What kind of life am I getting myself into?" she said aloud.

Chapter XIV

*George first visits the VA Hospital/
Trouble with Chris*

The following day, George went to the VA Hospital in West Haven for an appointment. It was the first time that he had been there, and he got lost driving. He had received the paperwork from the Motor Vehicle Company that had to be signed by his doctor. Driving was important to him, and the idea of not having a license bothered him.

"So you're moving your records from Minnesota to Connecticut?" the doctor asked. "Do you have any major problems?"

"I need to obtain a new driver's license. I have the paper work here for you to fill out."

"Oh, I'll be glad to do that for you," Dr. Ling said. "I notice that you are trembling a little, does this occur daily?"

"Yes. I have Parkinson's disease. I've had it for six years, but in the last month, I've begun to shake more than usual. I don't know just why."

"Do you have any other medical problems?"

"No. I don't think so. I had my eyes tested last week, and there was no problem with my vision. I've been driving all my life. I see no reason to stop now." George saw no reason to mention blood that was in his urine from time to time; the tinnitus that he had had for years; epilepsy that he had grown out of, or the fact that he wore hearing aids.

"Well, you probably will have no difficulty obtaining a Connecticut license. Make an appointment with Dr. Fisher when you leave. You should also set up an appointment with the neurologist, Dr. Guini, since you have Parkinson's disease. It's important to monitor how your drugs react."

"O.K," George said. "Is that all?"

"Yes, for now."

When he returned, George was in good spirits. "They told me not to worry about my license. I had to make some more appointments with two other doctors, but that's to be expected. Tomorrow, I'll call New London and talk to the cancer drug study people. West Haven doesn't handle that."

"You always get involved in drug studies, George. Why? You don't have cancer do you?" Emilia asked.

"No. I just want to make life easier for someone who does. They offered me the opportunity to participate, and I'm just helping them out."

"Well, you have to consider the transportation to New London. If you don't drive there, you can catch the train easily enough. But what if the drugs that you are testing cause side effects?"

"Why should they?"

"It happened to me when I was in the drug study for Vigabetrin. I wanted to commit suicide." Emilia replied. "You never can tell with drugs."

"That was you and an anticonvulsant." George said. His face showed the irritation that he felt. He began to wonder whether Emilia really wanted him around.

"It's your life," she replied as she left the room.

"Come back in here. Where are you going?"

"To work on the files, I need to get through with my part of the project. Anyway, what's left to talk about?"

In reply, George rose, put on his shoes, and hooking Pepper's leash to his collar, he walked out.

Emilia went to the office and continued working on the files. It seemed like an endless job. She had approximately four different manuscripts that were filed separately in the drawers, as well as a lot of little stuff. This project of re-filing the files was something that needed to be done, but now wasn't the time that she wanted to do it. Still, it would make things easier in the long run.

She heard George close the back door as Pepper came running into the room to greet her. He seemed excited and happy. Emilia knew that Pepper enjoyed the walks. She realized that in the last two years, she had cut his walks shorter and shorter. They no longer walked eight blocks. Since her fall in France earlier this summer, Emilia's back wasn't up to walking Pepper long distances. Usually she felt as though he were walking her.

"Hi Pepper. Where did you go? Did you have fun?" she asked patting his back. "George is a good friend of yours, isn't he?"

"He had fun watching the squirrels climbing the trees. He would try and chase them, but they would go into the tree. Then he just stood and looked at them," George said from the doorway. "It's getting a little breezy out, so we didn't stay as long as I'd like. What's for supper?"

"I haven't given that a thought. It's only three in the afternoon," Emilia replied. "How about soup and sandwiches," Emilia asked. "But you'll have to wait two hours or so for me to fix anything."

"That sounds good. I'll fix supper. You just work on the files." Turning on his heel, George left.

"I should have suggested that before now," Emilia said to herself.

For another hour, she continued to work undisturbed. Then a loud clatter from the kitchen brought her running out of the office. All of the pans below the coffee maker were on the floor. George was stooped down picking them up.

"Don't worry. I did it. I'll clean it up," he said.

"Fine."

Back in the office, she resumed her work. It was difficult to pay attention to what she wanted to do and still listen to hear if anything else had gone wrong. The TV was blaring, as usual. George had had tinnitus since she had first known him. When he got hearing aids, he refused to wear them. So, volume was always higher than she liked it. That hadn't changed. Emilia realized that she had lived this way once before and been unable to concentrate on anything. She also knew that her seizures occurred more frequently. She hadn't fallen, but the length of time that she remained in a confused state after a seizure had increased. There was no question that having a man around who required being watched was draining.

Suddenly, the fire alarm went off. It did this infrequently, but usually there was a cause. When she got to the kitchen, smoke was everywhere. The toaster had jammed, and George had unplugged it, but not before the room was saturated with smoke.

There was a loud knock on the back door, and Chris was yelling at George. "Don't you know how to make toast, you fool?"

"I know how to make toast, but the toaster jammed. It was an accident."

"I don't like accidents that happen and disturb me," Chris said. "Now the stupid alarm won't go off until the fire fighters come."

For once, Chris was giving the eleventh degree to someone else besides Emilia. Still, she felt responsible for the problem. He was her guest. When the fire fighters came, Emilia was told in no uncertain terms that she was responsible for George's actions. The alarm went off at anything. George had tried to stop it, and made it worse. That had really irritated Chris, who lived above them. Chris and his wife grew angry when anything that they didn't approve of occurred in Apartment B. Chris was a lawyer, and his wife Jo Lynn was a teacher. They had no children and no pets. They seemed to have a vendetta against Emilia and anyone who associated with her.

"How does it feel to have someone correct you?" Emilia asked George when they had returned to the apartment.

"I don't mind. I made a mistake. It could have caused a fire. It didn't." George said. "Chris seems like a responsible fellow."

"Responsible? Only you would say that. See if you still think that after living here a year." Emilia replied.

"Let's have supper." George said.

"Is the soup hot?"

"Yeah,"

"No it isn't," Emilia said when she took a sip of the soup. "It's cold. Where is the sandwich or whatever?"

"I'll heat it up, and get the sandwiches."

By now, George's hands were shaking so much the soup rolled in the mugs. He took them and placed them in the microwave. The sandwiches were made, but not on the table. Emilia helped him set the table. When they finally sat down to eat, Emilia realized that she missed the blessing that Moona always said. George waited for her to say grace. He rarely said it.

After supper, Emilia washed the dishes and was about to go back to the office when George insisted that she join him on the couch. "I need a little comfort from you," he said. Emilia had no choice but to sit down and let him kiss or slosh her. She called it 'slosh' because it was so liquid. She didn't tell him that. After a few minutes, he seemed satisfied and returned his attention to the TV. He kept her hand in his, so there was no point in leaving. Emilia thought to herself, "This is the way people act when they are married." But she didn't believe what she was thinking. Sometimes people on TV acted this way, but married folk? That was another story altogether.

They sat there watching TV and holding hands for a while. Finally, George's hands began to tremble again, and he let her hand go. It was evident that he wanted her to stay close by, though. In another twenty minutes, he had dropped off to sleep. Emilia slowly rose from the couch and returned to the office.

"I can't seem to stay awake anymore." George said from the doorway an hour later. "I'm taking a bath and going to bed."

"Fine, you looked worn out, so I let you sleep." Emilia replied. "I'll be along in a little while."

"O. K."

Emilia listened to George's footsteps as he walked. He had trouble picking his feet up. When he got home, he always took his shoes off, but he'd always done that. In Hawaii and Japan, it had been expected. Had Daniel had had all of these problems too? She knew that he probably had, but she didn't remember his nose and mouth leaking as George's did. She questioned whether or not the continual dripping was dangerous to his health.

Chapter XV

George and Emilia go to the VA hospital and talk with Bary about marriage

Things didn't change that much until late September when George received word that his request for a new license had been denied. Before that, he had spent a lot of time working on the car. He had cleaned, taped and glued the right hand mirror back on twice. He had finally gotten the glass to stay in the mount. This had taken a large part of the day, and kept him occupied. He enjoyed working with cars. That was one of his hobbies. George also enjoyed collecting coins. Today he got them out again, believing that he captivated Moona's and Nicole's attention with these miraculous coins.

"I can drive until the ninth of October," George had said when he opened the notice. "That gives us some time to take care of things that need to be done. I'll take the car down to Pet Boys tomorrow and have the radiator adjusted."

"Can you manage alright without a car, Dad?" Nicole asked from the doorway. She had just come over to borrow some eggs.

"Sure. I'll be O.K. I've taken the bus to the VA Hospital once already. Your mother insisted that I learn the bus route. And, you have a pull cart that is good for putting groceries in. I can take that on the bus to get the groceries."

"You don't have to bother about them. I'll take you and mother when you need to go shopping." Nicole promised. She knew that her father would be lost without a car, but it was better to have him alive and not driving than killed in a fatal accident. She, like her mother, was terrified when she rode with him.

"We have an appointment at the hospital next week," Emilia said. "Dad is supposed to see his neurologist, Dr. Guini. I've never been there on the bus."

"I can drop you out there, but you will have to take the bus home."

"That will work," Emilia said.

When the day came for the initial visit, George, Emilia, and Nicole went to the hospital. Nicole wasn't used to going there, but she soon learned her way. "Would you like to stay and have lunch with us?" George said.

"Sure."

They found the cafeteria and ordered three Rubens. Nicole and George especially liked Rubens and you didn't see them that much in Connecticut. While they ate, they talked about the hospital. George was very impressed with the service that he had gotten so far. Emilia liked the camaraderie that she felt around military hospitals. George paid for the meals and Emilia and Nicole carried the trays. It had taken a while to get their order, for everyone seemed to be ordering the same thing. After lunch, Nicole took off, and Emilia and George went back to the waiting room. Emilia had her new book and her Mary Kay samples with her, as always. She also had a newspaper to read.

After George signed in, they sat down and waited. The neurologist took her time about making an appearance. First, they were sent to an anti-room where a psychologist talked to George. Then, they were taken to another room to await Dr. Guini.

When she appeared, she seemed quite affable. She looked at George and then told them both that Parkinson's was a difficult disease to handle. It was necessary to have the right medication to make it work. She didn't make any changes, but suggested that George discontinue the medication that he had been taking for the drug study.

* * *

When they left, it didn't take long to get the bus. They stopped back in down town New Haven and made a call on Bary, the minister. Emilia had almost forgotten that the appointments were the same day. Bary asked them if they were still arguing, or if they had made any changes.

"I'm not driving after October 9th," George said. "I feel badly about that because I had promised Emilia that I would take her anywhere she needed to go. But she seems to be adjusting to it alright."

"Is that right, Emilia? How do you feel about George losing his license?"

"Relieved."

"Why?"

"George would never admit it, but he has trouble driving. I've been afraid for a long time that he would have another accident." Emilia pointed out. "Maybe this is a blessing in disguise."

"That's a good way to look at it," Bary said. "Did he take you out on the town, as I suggested?"

"Not really. He hasn't felt that well. Many of the places we would like to go to require driving at night. I didn't ask to be taken out, and he didn't take me out."

"I've been spending a lot of time walking the dog and letting Emilia work."

"Do you think that you want to marry George now, Emilia?"

"No. We're arguing too much. I am turning back into an old hag."

"I never said that," George said.

"That isn't all. It's hard for me to sleep with him. The bed feels like a roller-coaster ride. I haven't adjusted to that." Emilia closed her eyes as she spoke. She should have added that George made her wonder if Daniel would have been the same way. No one would know the answer to that, least of all these two men.

"Well, it looks as though we're still waiting to set a date," Bary said.

"There is nothing in the world that would make me happier than to marry Emilia today," George said.

"I'm sure that you are sincere, George. But marriage is a two-way street. Apparently, Emilia has some reservations that she needs to overcome. See you in a month."

Ushering them out of the office, Bary wondered to himself just what could happen to change Emilia's mind.

Section VI:

October-December 2004

Chapter XVI

Hallucinations begin

Emilia and George left in silence. When they got to the corner, George suggested that they walk over to an Oriental Restaurant that everyone kept passing by. Emilia thought that was an excellent idea. As they walked, he began to talk.

"Why do we have to marry in the church? Couldn't we just go to the Justice of the Peace and have a civil ceremony? It would be faster, and probably cheaper."

"George, I don't want to marry you. I like you as a friend. It's taken us a long time to develop a friendship. We never had it when we were married."

"Have another boy friend?"

"Certainly not! What type of person do you think I am?"

"You tell me."

"Quit trying to start an argument." When Emilia got angry, she walked faster. At least, now she and George were walking side by side in silence.

It took them about ten more minutes to reach the Oriental restaurant on Trumbull Street. When they got there, George went back to the back to find a waitress. While Emilia waited, she walked around and looked at the pottery that was for sale. She found some that she liked, and decided that she would come back and get it later. Soon, they were seated at a cozy little table for two. There were two other couples there also. Out of habit, Emilia looked at the prices first. She found something that sounded good for a reasonable price. As usual, George ordered a dish that was more expensive. Emilia decided that this time, she'd change her mind and would have something of equal value. George seemed a little surprised that she had changed her order, but he gave no impression of being upset.

As they began to eat and talk, Emilia relaxed. The food was good. She used her chopsticks expertly. George had asked for silverware. He told her that he had trouble holding chopsticks now. Emilia realized that the disease was getting to him.

When George had paid the bill, they left just in time to catch the last bus out of New Haven. It was about 9:35 at night. The wind had come up and it looked as though rain was coming. Emilia was relieved to see the bus.

"You take the dog out when we get home," George said on the bus. "I'm too tired." Reaching into his pocket, George pulled out the keys and gave it to her.

Surprised, Emilia accepted them without comment.

When they got to the apartment, Pepper was ready to leave. Emilia fed him, and then took him out for his evening walk. She was glad to have the keys back. Lately, Nicole had found them in the outside door on two occasions. Emilia was beginning to wonder how she could persuade George to let her have the key. They took a longer walk than usual. When they got back, George was just getting out of the tub. A few minutes later, he was sitting beside her on the couch, with only shorts and a tee shirt.

"Aren't you cold?" Emilia asked.

"No. I turned the heat up. I'm fine."

"Where is that nice brown house coat that you bought in Hong Kong years ago?"

"Your son-in-law took it."

"Which one," Emilia asked.

"Yenta's husband, Lothar," George replied

"Oh, that's too bad." Emilia replied, secretly wondering how much credibility to place in his story. She knew that he didn't like their son-in-law. He had accused him of many things over the years. Yet, Yenta and Theo had been married since 1989. Theo wasn't very dependable in Emilia's view, but Yenta seemed to love him.

"Come closer to me," George said as he put his arm around her.

"I'm as close as I can get."

"No. You're still trying to read that paper." George said as he took it from her and kissed her.

"I thought that you said you were tired."
"I am, but I'm hungry too."
"We just ate."
"For you."
"Oh." Emilia felt a little panic stricken.

After he had made love to her, she wondered again if he was interested in her as a person, or just a free ride with sex and care thrown in. He'd always said that when he retired, he wanted to be a bum and travel the world. It was evident to Emilia that his body was in no shape to travel extensively, but she wondered just how 'intimate' he really wanted her to be. Every time that he took her in his arms, she thought of Daniel. She had felt the Parkinson's tremble first when he held her in his arms and all that she could feel was bones, no fat. George's bones felt even frailer than Daniel's had. She wondered just how long she could live with him. Yet, she realized that she liked being held by a man, even this man who had hurt her so much. As he let her go, she noticed that he was losing his urine. She wasn't too surprised. She remembered all the times she had lost urine after seizures that changed into tonic-clonic seizures.

That night, when they went to bed, he was up and down five times. In the morning, he asked her if they could switch sides of the bed. Emilia didn't like the right hand side because she had to sleep on her right side. She agreed to switch, however; for it was evident that he had problems getting to the bathroom in time. Moona had noticed how badly the bathroom smelled the last time that she was over. In fact, she had cleaned the toilet bowl out to get rid of 'Grandpa's stink.'

The following night, George went to bed early, but by eight o'clock, he was circling the living room in his tee shirt and underpants holding a flashlight. He looked near the fireplace, beside the TV, by the piano. Emilia watched him, puzzled by his actions.

"What are you looking for?"
"Don't you see them?"
"No. What are you talking about?"
"Can't you see the blue people over by the fireplace? They're eating Chocolate Chip cookies and talking."
"Can you hear what they are saying?" Emilia asked. She realized that he was fantasizing, and decided to play along to see what he would say.
"No. They only talk to themselves." George looked a little frightened by the people. He kept going around the room.

"George, there are no people. It is just your imagination."

George reached out to grasp a person, but nothing was there. Without saying anymore, he left the room.

Emilia had just started a good book, and she had no intention of going to bed. An hour later, he was back with the flashlight again. This time, he sat down on the couch and accused her of having a boyfriend in the room.

"Is he blue?" Emilia asked.

"No. Your boyfriend is brown."

"What happened to the blue people?" she asked.

"Oh, they're still over there," he said pointing toward an old secretary that had belonged to her great-grandmother.

"Are they still eating cookies?"

"One of them is."

"George, we are going to have to go back to the VA Hospital if you continue to see people. There is no one here but you, me and the dog." As Emilia spoke, she placed her hand on his arm in an attempt to reassure him that everything would be all right.

"OK."

"Maybe it's the medicine that you are taking. Are you still taking that stuff for the drug study?"

"Yes."

"Maybe you should just take the drugs for the Parkinson's disease."

"Maybe, I'm going back to bed." Turning the light off, he left the room.

Emilia continued to read for a little while longer, then took a bath and went to bed. It was difficult to sleep facing him, watching the salivation stream from his mouth and nose. But she had no choice. It hurt her hip to sleep on the other side, and she snored if she lay on her back.

Suddenly, George sat up in bed. Then he lay back down and stopped trembling for a moment.

I suppose this is only the beginning of the problems we'll have, Emilia thought to herself

* * *

The following day, Emilia went to see her attorney Patrick. She had made an appointment to go over her own will. George had shown her a form that he had been given in Minnesota, and he told her that he would fill it out. Emilia doubted whether he would, as his writing was deteriorating rapidly. Patrick's uncle had had Parkinson's disease, and he understood it better than Emilia. While she was there going over the will, and making changes in the names of her grandchildren, they talked about the side effects of Parkinson's disease. Patrick was concerned about Emilia. He knew how she had felt about his uncle, and it was evident that she was caught in a bind by George's actions.

"Have you considered looking at what alternatives you have?"

"What do you mean?"

"Well, it's evident that he can't continue to drive much longer. I have the name of a home in northern Connecticut for Veterans. Maybe you should apply there. At least, give them a call and see what it is like."

"You're a good friend."

"I don't like seeing you this upset, Emilia. George can't expect you or Nicole to take care of him indefinitely. It's not feasible."

"Oh, but he does. I just don't know whether I can handle his hallucinations."

"They have started?"

"Yes. It's like living in a fantasy world." Emilia said. "I have no control of what is going on in his mind. Neither does George."

"That's pretty accurate. That is another reason that you have to start planning how you will deal with this in the future. As long as you aren't married, you're OK, but if you were to marry, you'd be in an entirely different situation. It would be much worse."

"You're probably correct." Emilia said. "I don't see any chance of that occurring."

"Good."

As she left the office, Emilia realized how important Patrick's friendship was. He had told her that he would be through with her will in a week or so. She should make an appointment to see him next week. He'd also suggested that George should make a will soon.

Chapter XVII

Emilia hangs pictures at Claire's

On the first of October, a Saturday, George dropped Emilia off at *Claire's*. He hadn't been able to park the car, so he got her and the device he had put together to carry the pictures out and left. Emilia was afraid that the glass would break within the frames in George's carry-all. Luckily, that hadn't occurred.

She had arrived early, and done everything alone, placing the brackets on the beam near the ceiling, stringing the wire on them and the pictures and then standing back to be sure that they were straight. Emilia had had to buy wire that morning in order to hang all of the pictures. *Claire's* had had only a small amount of wire. When Emilia had hung pictures before, there had been nails to hang the pictures on each wall. Now, nails were only on one wall. Emilia remembered which pictures hung best at different heights; however, when she had reached the walls that demanded the brackets and wire, she had had to go slowly to keep from falling.

At 11:00 a.m., Mr. Beasley told her that she would have to leave because the lunch crowd was coming in. It was getting crowded. He told her to come back around three in the afternoon to finish.

This suited Emilia fine, as she would need a ladder to finish and none seemed available. Placing the four pictures that she still hadn't hung in the pull cart, Emilia headed for the bus. She tried to call Nicole and let her know that she would need her help around three. If someone had to climb a ladder, she had rather it be Nicole than herself. She had climbed on chairs and stepstools all morning long. Sometimes, she had wondered why she hadn't fallen. Before she left, she had a cup of coffee and rested before venturing out into the weather. It had begun to rain, and the wind was blowing the beautiful autumn leaves from the trees.

George was pleased that she had used his device for pulling the pictures. She told him that it worked. She didn't tell him how heavy it was to lift on and off of the bus. Even with just four pictures, it was a problem. When she had had it packed she had barely been able to lift it from his car. Although he had offered to do it for her, she trusted herself more than him.

About two-thirty, she headed back. This time, there were only four pictures, so she put them in a plastic bag from one of the local art stores to protect them from the rain and carried them easily. Just as she reached the corner where Claire's was located, she saw Nicole waving at her. Nicole hadn't gotten her message, but remembered that she had said something about three o'clock when they talked last night. They went into the quiet restaurant. One of the waiters found a ladder, and offered to help. With three of them working, it took all of twenty minutes to do everything. Although they weren't as straight as she would have liked, the pictures were hung.

Emilia and Nicole were relieved. Mrs. Beasley had asked for a book that contained all the pictures and their prices. She didn't tell Emilia where to place it, so she gave it to the waiter, and told him to put it on the shelf in the kitchen. Emilia understood that later Mrs. Beasley would put it out where people could look at it. She wondered what had happened to the copy of her new book that she had left with Mrs. Beasley in September.

Emilia and Nicole left the restaurant. As they were leaving, Emilia had a seizure in which she was only confused. However, Nicole noticed it and asked her mother if anything were wrong. When she got no answer, she knew that Emilia was in trouble. After two minutes, Emilia was fine and asked Nicole if she had done anything wrong.

"No. You just had a little seizure. You wouldn't answer me."

"I couldn't talk. I'm sorry."

"You don't need to be sorry. Dad's upsetting you, isn't he?"

"Well, yes. He keeps seeing these people who don't exist. It's all I can do to keep my sanity. Nicole, you have no idea how difficult it is to live with him."

"I can imagine." Nicole answered. "Mother, you have to take care of yourself. You've come so far, you can't go back to the way you were before you came to Connecticut."

"I don't want to. Sometimes I feel as though I am acting like his slave again. Other times, I feel like an old hag who harps upon someone who doesn't do everything perfectly. And yet, I feel responsible for his being here. I'm the one who pushed for getting married."

"No. He pushed marriage. Remember the letter that you sent him last year?"

"The one that he claims he never received?"

"Yes. I watched you mail it." Nicole said. "My money says he got it and tore it up."

"I wouldn't be surprised if you are right. Thanks honey." Emilia reached over and hugged Nicole. "We better get going."

When they arrived at home, it was almost four-thirty. George was beside himself with worry. His hallucinations had kicked in again and he was beginning to wonder where she had gone. Nicole stopped in just long enough to help her mother bring in the wire cutters and paper bag that she had taken with her. She wanted to be sure that she was all right.

"Where have you been? I've been worried sick about you, Emilia."

"I went back to hang pictures. It took longer than I thought it would."

"With Nicole helping, I doubt it."

"How have you been?"

"The blue people have come back. I can't get them to leave."

Emilia wished that suddenly, things were back to normal and she had time to paint. Moona and Nicole were still living there, or at least visiting more than they did. She asked herself again whether she should marry George or not. When she had talked to Reba last week, Reba had encouraged her to re-marry. "There is a reason for it." She had said.

Whatever the reason, Emilia knew that marriage would be difficult. She missed having the girls nearby or phoning. Nowadays, Moona kept a low profile. George didn't like her friend Tessa and made no bones about it. This combined with the wary feeling her Grandfather gave her, made Moona stay away as much as possible.

Something had happened when she was a small child that still troubled her. She and her friends spent as little time as possible around her grandparents. Emilia missed seeing them, yet she enjoyed not having everyone's children under foot. She couldn't understand why George was so critical of Moona's friend Tessa. Tessa and Moona were inseparable. Last year, Moona had had more friends over all of the time.

Nicole liked Tessa, and apparently, Tessa's mother liked Moona. George couldn't understand why anyone would want to associate with someone who wore tattoos as she did. Tessa's tattoos were painted on, but they didn't wash off easily. George didn't seem to care; he disapproved. Nicole kept her tattoos well hidden.

Emilia began to fix supper. It was that time of day, and she had to keep herself busy and keep George's mind occupied with other things besides hallucinations. That night they had a quiet supper and watched TV. George dozed off on the couch and then woke up and talked for a while, before dozing off again. As usual his conversations included information about what 'should have' been done or what they 'had done' in past years. George had difficulty focusing his thoughts on the present. They dealt more with the past. Finally at eight, he took a bath and went to bed. He seemed to sleep rather well. Emilia guessed that he was tired.

The following day, a Sunday, he dressed and got the car out. His license was still good, so he decided that they would go to the church on the Green. When they arrived, Emilia had to usher. George sat towards the front of the church in his usual place. He looked so forlorn that Emilia began to feel guilty. After church, they drove to *Windy's* and had the *senior special*, Chili and a salad. For 99 cents, who could go wrong? Emilia noticed that lately George had had more and more trouble eating. Today, he had to manipulate his utensils with his left hand, which was awkward for him, but safer if he wished to eat the food. If the food were held in his right hand, half of it went on the floor. She remembered Daniel having similar problems with pens.

If they were at home, Pepper cleaned up the mess, but when they were out, George was on his own. Emilia was glad that they were going to see the neurologist soon. It would be a relief to know whether the wrong medication was causing the hallucinations. Emilia watched George as he maneuvered the fork and knife that he'd been given. He didn't seem to be concerned over the mess that he made, only that the food went into his mouth. During the last month, she'd noticed that he ate faster and faster, as though food would suddenly become unavailable. George had always eaten a lot, but recently he seemed to swallow it before he had chewed it. One of the people that had seen him at the VA, a speech therapist, had sent her a note telling her to make him eat with his head level with the table, instead of hanging down, and insist that he chew his food well. She'd suggested both, but he had paid her little mind. Emilia was still eating her own food, when George looked up and asked her when she would be through.

"I'm not in a hurry, George. We have the rest of the day."

"I want to go home. Will you hurry up?" he said impatiently.

Emilia took her time finishing the Chili, and drinking the coffee that she had ordered. George had spent too much of his life ordering her around, she wasn't going to give him the satisfaction of continuing to do so. She was glad that the following evening she had her Mary Kay Meeting. It would get her out of the house without George. That would be a relief.

Chapter XVIII

VA Hospital's ER/Neurologist

    The next evening, Emilia told George that she would take the key with her to the meeting. She had been leaving it at home and letting him use it as he pleased; but tonight she wanted to get in when she rang the bell. Lately, he had quit using his hearing aid and generally never heard the bell. Their director had moved the meeting to another location that week, as the old location was being redone. Jana picked her up early, and they had a pleasant visit with one of Jana's new recruits. By the time that they arrived, Emilia was hungry. There were some crackers, cheese and juice. The new place had specific rules, and it was necessary to leave at exactly 8:30. That worked out better for some of the people. Others would have enjoyed a longer meeting. There were about eight regular people, and four who only came occasionally. Since Halloween was the next holiday, Zena, one of the Mary Kay directors, had made baskets that depicted the holiday. Everyone was interested in the way she had made them. However, no one had really sold a great amount of products and there was a three-way tie between Lena, Lilly, and Jay. After this, they left. Jana had another appointment to go to. She dropped Emilia at home around 8:45 p.m.

    When Emilia opened the door, Pepper was barking hysterically. Every bark produced a zap from his 'no bark' collar that should have made any dog stop; but Pepper only continued to bark and moan. Emilia took his collar off, walked the dog, and he quieted down. After she returned from the walk, she heard no sound of George, and began to wonder where he was. As she was hanging up her coat, George and one of the neighbors in another section of the building came in.

"Why, you're home! Emilia." Matt said. "George has been over at my place for the past hour. He wanted to call the police. He keeps saying that there are cars in the back, a boat-car, movie equipment, and a lot of other stuff."

"He has been having hallucinations lately. I think that they may be caused by the medication that he takes." Emilia said.

"Well, you better do something about him soon. We can't have people who visit here wandering around."

"Yes, I agree with you." Emilia replied. She didn't know Matt; but appreciated the fact that she had brought George back home. "He probably locked himself out. I took the key with me tonight, because I thought that I would be back later. Thanks for bringing George home."

"See that it doesn't happen again." Matt replied.

Emilia wondered what they expected her to do. Soon the phone was ringing and another neighbor was suggesting that perhaps she should take him to the emergency ward at the hospital. Emilia respected Laura's expertise and they talked for a while. She agreed that she couldn't have someone living there who hallucinated constantly and bothered the neighbors. But even as she said this, Emilia realized that people were more concerned about their own comfort than her husband's health. She had always wondered if she had had a seizure and been alone, would anyone notice? Probably not, she thought; no one from the condo ever checked in on her except Laura.

George hadn't said very much. He might have listened to what she was saying on the phone, but Emilia couldn't tell.

"George, what really did happen?" she asked.

"It began again. First, it was only the blue people, then when I looked out the back window there was an entire movie crew out by the garage making a movie of aliens. Some of them were blue, some green. There were so many cars, and even more people. I began to wonder if we were being invaded. Then the sides of the garage began to crumble. That's when I went next door to call the police." George said. "Nobody believed me. But I saw everything, Emilia. I'm not making anything up."

"I believe you, George. I believe that you did see all of this, but I am willing to bet that either your medication is causing this, or it is a side-effect of Parkinson's disease." Emilia said calmly.

"What can we do?"

"I am going to call a taxi, and we are going to the VA Hospital and find out what is wrong."

"I'd like that."

Emilia called a cab, took out her last $20.00, and prayed that it would be enough. Nicole was working tonight, so she could probably pick them up. Emilia had gone out there on her own earlier in the month to talk with George's Social Worker. Everyone had liked her book, and it had been a pleasant afternoon. Tonight was different. The cab driver lost no time in getting to the hospital, after Emilia said they were going to the Emergency Room. The fare was $14.00. Emilia waited impatiently for the $6.00 change.

It took a while to register, but just as they sat down and began to take off their coats, someone came for George. Emilia was told to remain in the waiting room until she was called. In ten minutes, someone came for her and the coats that she was carrying. When she got to the ER, George was lying on a bed, drinking water. An IV was connected to his arm. He looked relaxed for a change. One of the ER doctors called the on-call neurologist to assess the problem. They took pictures of George's lungs, tried unsuccessfully to get a urine sample, and kept handing him a glass of water to drink. He shook when he held it in his right hand and spilled it all over himself which made him cold. Finally, Emilia went over and held it for him.

"I keep having shooting pains from my feet to my knees." George said. This was a new complaint to Emilia, although she remembered that eighteen years ago George had complained that his legs had no feeling. She had thought that odd at the time.

When asked, George told them all of the drugs that he was taking except the drugs for the cancer study.

"Don't forget the drug study," she chided.

"One of the drugs that you are taking for Parkinson's can cause hallucinations, Mr. Blake. "We need to get you off of that tonight and any other drugs aside from the Parkinson's drugs." Dr. Joe said. "How does that sound. Can you do that?"

"Fine, I'll do anything to keep from seeing those people." George replied.

"You told us that there were movie actors dressed like aliens outside the house. Did they talk?"

"They talked to each other, but I couldn't understand what they said."

"How long did this go on?" As he spoke, the orderly began to move around the table and check George's legs and feet. "Does that hurt?" he asked as he ran a finger under his foot.

"About an hour, and yes it hurts." George said. "Emilia had left, and the blue people stayed there until she came back."

"How long were you gone, Mrs. Blake?"

"Emilia?" George said.

"Emilia, how long were you gone?"

Emilia snapped back to reality, she had been a little dizzy. "I was gone from 6:00 to 8:45 p.m. When I came home, he was at a neighbor's home trying to call the police for help," she said. "I had no idea that the hallucinations had escalated to such a degree. Before, they were just people who came into the living room every night. Now, we seem to have an entire scenario."

"This happens sometimes." Dr. Joe said. "Parkinson's is a difficult disease to diagnose and control. It affects the entire body. I want to take him off Mylar, and order a new medication for him. I'm making an appointment for him to see one of our best neurologists next week."

"Good." Emilia said. Suddenly, she looked at the clock and saw that it was nearing twelve. "I need to call our daughter to pick us up."

"You will have to go outside the door and make the call. We aren't through yet, though." Dr. Joe continued. "I want more x-rays of his chest, and some cream for his feet."

Emilia left through the door that Dr. Joe had indicated and called Nicole at the hospital. Nicole was just leaving when she answered.

"Why are you at the hospital, Mother? Did something happen to Dad? Is he alright?" Nicole asked.

"Your father's hallucinations have grown worse. It's probably only the medication. They are changing that. We need you to come and pick us up. Can you do that? I don't think that they are quite ready." she added.

"I'm on my way," Nicole replied.

Although Nicole got there quickly, it was another hour and a half before they finally were dismissed from the ER. Everyone was relieved that Nicole had come to pick up her parents. One of the people in the ER knew Nicole, as they both worked at Yale-New Haven Hospital. This was only the first of many nights that Nicole would pick up her parents at a hospital.

* * *

When it was time for George to see Dr. Guini at the VA Hospital, Nicole drove her parents there and stayed with them. George saw a psychiatrist before he saw the neurologist that day. Emilia's first reaction to the neurologist was positive. Dr. Guini told her that another friend had published a book through Xlibris Corporation and done quite well. Then turning her attention to George, she noted that the hallucinations hadn't gotten better, just more vivid and there were more and more scenarios. They had gone from blue people to entire casts or characters. They usually started later in the evening. Removing one of the Parkinson drugs had helped, but it hadn't solved the problem. Rather than adding the drug that had been recommended by the ER doctor, she left him on only Carbadopa-Lavadopa. George seemed satisfied, yet puzzled.

"Do you have any questions?"

"I do." George said.

"What is it?" answered the neurologist.

"I would like for you to place me in the hospital for two days and diagnose what is wrong with me. I want to know why I am seeing these people." George said.

"Hallucinations are a part of the disease, George. I see no reason to put you in the hospital. You're not sick. I'd rather treat you as an out patient."

"I think that he should be put in the hospital. What happens if he has a reaction to the medication?"

"He won't."

Rather than say anymore, Emilia turned and left the room. George followed. Later, they went to visit the Social Worker. Emilia had received the paperwork from the Veteran's Home in northern Connecticut. Ms. Black helped them fill out the material and suggested that Nicole drive them up to look at it. She also had George sign a living will, and another form that required a notary public's assistance. Ms. Black suggested that if they could, they should visit the Veteran's Home in Rocky Hill as soon as possible. Then, they were off. George wanted to go grocery shopping, so they stopped in West Haven at Adam's Supermarket. Nicole and George were surprised when Emilia's prediction of lower prices proved true. They hadn't shopped there before.

Chapter XIX

George and Emilia get married

To try and get her mind off of George and his problems, she talked to the publishing company and ordered more books to show at the up-coming book signing. Every opportunity Emilia had, she showed her book. She made about eight sales before the book signing on November first. A couple of them were in Boston. She had sent one book to Edinborough, Scotland where one of her friends planned to show it at the European Congress on Children with Cerebral Palsy. Milo had shown her work in Nice, several years earlier. Emilia had met him in 1989 in Prague.

Emilia continued to feel guilty because George's disorder was taking so much of her time. She felt as though she was becoming an old hag whom he ordered around at his pleasure. He was constantly telling her that it was time to fix some meal. Her life was no longer her own. However, the only way that she could think of solving the problem was to marry George.

That, she believed would make him happy. The object was to enjoy his company. The fact that this was becoming harder didn't seem to be a factor she could change. She had ordered the marketing material from Xlibris, and set up the date for the book signing on November 1, 2004. There hadn't been a great deal of time in October for her to go by *Claire's* and see if the pictures were selling. George had begun to occupy all of her time. His drooling had increased to the point that he leaked saliva and nasal residue constantly. He continued to hold his head over, and so his clothes stayed wet. So did the floor and the couch. She tried to tell herself that she was getting used to it, but truthfully, she hated it. Even Pepper tried to dodge his drooling.

On the 23rd of October, Emilia slept on the couch. It wasn't the first time, and wouldn't be the last. George took all of the covers off. He still insisted that she sleep on the far side of the bed. He was getting up six or seven times a night. All of these things added to no sleep at night. Emilia thought that something besides Parkinson's disease was wrong. So did her daughter, Nicole. The question was what?

Emilia felt sorry for George. Sometimes he could be so dear, and then other times he seemed to expect the world to revolve around him. Emilia still couldn't carry on a conversation with him that didn't involve his coin collection, how she should change, the TV analyst Dr. Phil, or his views on the annual Navy Reunion. When she had invited him to go with her to the annual meeting of the American Epilepsy Society in New Orleans in December, he had declined, saying that he'd prefer to save the money and go to Milwaukee for the reunion. He offered to pay for Emilia's ticket, but told her to go by herself. Although she planned to visit their daughter Leah, he didn't want to go.

On October 27th, George and Emilia were married at the New Haven City Hall. Some people wondered why Emilia wanted to marry George, but they discreetly said nothing. Others knew that Emilia married George because she believed that she loved him and she wanted to care for him. Still others knew that she had other reasons as well.

George bought a new pair of shoes for the ceremony. Emilia wore a spring dress that she had bought earlier. Afterwards, Emilia, Nicole, Moona and George went to the new Japanese restaurant that George and Emilia liked in Hamden. The food was good, and everyone was relaxed and happy.

On the 31st, Emilia took all of her pictures down from *Claire's*. She picked up the book, which had never moved off of the kitchen shelf, therefore never been available to the clients. Nicole helped her take the pictures down and bring them home. Only one person was interested in a picture. However, she never contacted Emilia. The following night, November 1st, Emilia set up her books or a circular table near the front door of the restaurant. Three of her good friends did come by. Books were shown, and marketing material was arranged in an interesting manner. Although, Emilia didn't have a lot of people come to the book signing, she was happy that she'd had the chance to have it.

George hadn't come to the book signing either. It was as though he didn't want to go out unless it was something that he suggested. It had always been that way. Emilia wondered why she had believed that he would change. She had hoped against hope that they could be happy. Emilia realized that there were times when she felt sorry for George, and she wondered if this feeling were masquerading as love. It had happened before. Perhaps it wasn't love, but the desire to be a helpmate that permeated her desire to be his wife. She wondered how she would get through the next day. Reba was conspicuous by her absence from the scene.

Chapter XX

*George stops sleeping in bed and sleeps on the couch.
He can not sleep under covers*

George developed a phobia about sleeping under covers. He had more and more difficulty crawling into the bed. When he got into bed, he crawled in on his knees, and then rolled over into a fetal position entangling his feet in the covers. Because his knees remained bent in a sitting position, he began to walk about and lie in bed with them bent. This made it difficult to sleep in bed. He couldn't sleep with covers over him. This created a problem at night because Emilia needed covers during the night. To resolve the problem, he had begun sleeping on top of the sheets, but with the furnace turned on high. Emilia was too hot to sleep.

Later, that week, it was evident that George didn't feel comfortable sleeping in bed with Emilia. He couldn't control his urine, and opted to sleep on the couch. This seemed to be the only place that he felt comfortable. George's body had developed a severe curvature that made sleeping in reclining positions impossibility.

When they went to the hospital in November, for George's usual appointment, Dr. Guini added gabapentin (Neurontin) to counteract the shooting pains that he felt in his legs and feet. She hoped that this would enable him to sleep through the night. Instead, it gave him insomnia. It was to be titrated over a three-week period, with George increasing the dose by 100mg each week. One of the side effects was to exacerbate his tremor. By the end of the second week, George shook so much that he couldn't hold a fork or spoon. Emilia questioned the doctor's reasons for using this drug. George believed that they should continue to gradually increase the drug as Dr. Guini had suggested. The third week occurred the first week in December when Emilia would be traveling. She was concerned about what would happen in her absence.

* * *

Thanksgiving passed quietly, as Emilia and George hosted Nicole and Moona. Emilia stuffed the duck with her special cornbread dressing as Moona had requested. Nicole and Moona brought sweet potatoes, greens, and Nicole's special salad. They also found some Hawaiian dinner rolls. They ate early because Nicole had to work later in the day. Everyone enjoyed the meal. At that point, George's tremors were still under good control.

Once he had increased the gabapentin to 200 mg, Emilia had to feed him when he was tired. He couldn't hold a spoon at all. His feet began to swell so that they were unusually large. It became difficult for him to wear his old shoes, and almost impossible to wear his new ones.

When George was at home, he never wore shoes, just his socks. It was something that he had picked up from living in Hawaii and being in Japan during his Navy career. When you came into a house, you took off your outdoor shoes and wore house slippers.

George and Emilia went to his appointment with Dr. Joe on the second of December. He was concerned by the fact that George would be alone much of the time when Emilia was gone. She would be gone thirteen days. He sent them to ER with a request for admission. However, the admitting doctor refused his order, maintaining that George would only die of pneumonia if he remained there.

Emilia grew very angry with the doctor.

"Do you know anything about epilepsy?" she asked.

"Yes."

"Do you realize that putting pressure on people can cause them to have seizures?"

"Yes. But George doesn't have epilepsy. What is your point?"

"My point, sir, is that I have epilepsy. I am about to have a seizure because of your attitude. I am leaving now to eat something. But I will be back."

Emilia left and eventually found the dining facility. One of the men who knew how to work the machines that usually stole her money helped her get a sack of chips. She sat there and ate them, as she wondered where she was. The complex partial seizures that Emilia suffered from lasted only moments; but they could be very subtle. Picking up the cell phone, Emilia dialed her daughter.

"Nicole? Can you pick me up at the ER of the VA Hospital?"

"When, you don't sound so good."

"Now I just had a little seizure, not much. But your father is staying overnight. I don't believe that they will keep him longer than that. The doctor tried, but the admitting doctor is a twerp."

"Mother, remember we are leaving at four in the morning for the airport. I'll pick you up as soon as I get off, in about thirty minutes." Nicole said.

"I know. I have most of my bag packed. It won't take much longer. I'll be ready. Believe me I am upset that they won't keep your father any longer than overnight." Emilia replied.

"I don't like your seizures increasing this way."

"Neither do I," Emilia said.

"You need a break from taking care of Dad. He's hard for you to handle."

"I agree. I'll see you soon." Turning the cell phone off, Emilia sighed, as she turned to return to the ER. Nicole had a good point. She was exhausted. They had been at the hospital since noon. It was now nearing 11:00 pm. The nurse was still giving George water when she returned. Obtaining a urine sample tonight was important as George had complained about blood in his urine, as well as his swollen feet.

"Nicole is coming after me soon. You need to drink some more water for the nurse," Emilia said.

"I don't know why they won't let me stay here and find out why I am having so much trouble. I fought for my country. You'd think they don't even care about veterans, the service that you get here." George sulked. "I even asked the neurologist to hospitalize me for two days and find out what is the matter. I don't believe they care, Emilia."

"They're overcrowded, apparently." Emilia said.

When Nicole arrived, Emilia was ready to leave. They drove home in silence. When they got to the house, Nicole reminded her mother again to get some sleep and be ready when she came for her.

Chapter XXI

Emilia travels to New Orleans and Austin

Emilia spent most of the night packing and un-packing her bag. She would be spending six days in New Orleans at the American Medical Society's Annual meeting before going on to visit her daughter Leah and family in Austin. Emilia knew the weather could be either hot or cold, depending on whether there was wind. She had to pack for both. She was taking nine copies of her new book with her to display and sell, as well as Christmas presents. It took a little bit of pushing and pulling to get everything in. That didn't leave a lot of room for clothes. She took the essentials, which included her watercolours.

When Nicole picked her up, she was ready. The dog would be by himself today. Nicole would pick George up tomorrow at the hospital and bring him home. Pepper and George would have to take care of one another until she returned. She hoped that they could. Emilia gave Nicole the phone number of a nurses' assistant whom she had met on the bus. She had indicated that she could come in four hours a day if George needed help. Nicole took the information, but said nothing.

For the third of December, it was warmer than usual in Connecticut. Nicole dropped Emilia and her bag off at Continental Airlines after making her promise to call her when she got to New Orleans. Moona and Nicole would keep an eye on George and Pepper. Moona would stop in after school, and Nicole would stop in before and after work. Since Nicole worked two different shifts, she wasn't always available at the same times. Emilia hoped that George would be able to manage.

The flight was uneventful, and before long, Emilia was stepping off the plane in New Orleans. For 41 degrees, it was cold, as she had known it would be. The Gulf coast is damp, and the area around New Orleans and Houston can sound a lot warmer than it actually is. The Concierge at the hotel told her that she dressed like a native.

"Well, I was brought up just outside of Houston. I know what this weather is like," she replied with a smile.

Emilia hadn't been to New Orleans since 1958, the year that her grandmother had died. It was a beautiful city, and she had an enjoyable visit. However, she called Reba and Nicole constantly. Reba was helping her with a project that she was working on, and Nicole's impressions of George's actions were important for her to know. Emilia also talked to Ellie, the nurse's assistant she had met on the bus. Nicole believed that four hours of help wouldn't be enough. At ten dollars an hour, the price would become high after thirteen days of a six-hour shift, which was all that the girl now said she would consider.

The book seemed to go over well with several of the leading doctors. Emilia sent a copy to Australia with one of her acquaintances. The Epilepsy Society of Australia had purchased her last book on epilepsy, and they would be shown this one as well. The information available on epilepsy at the conference was new. The American Epilepsy Society conference also dealt with periventricular heterotopia, the disorder that had killed Leah's youngest son. There was a lot of material on genetics as well.

The last night Emilia attended a dinner at a nearby Omni hotel. She was a little late, and wound up sitting at the table with drug representatives from London, England. The pharmaceutical company was providing the dinner and the program on a new drug. Some of the people from England seemed interested in her new book. The hotel was quaint and more like New Orleans than the one where she was staying. The street was packed with antique shops and restaurants that were closed to Emilia's chagrin as she loved antiques.

The following day she made the short flight to Austin, and soon saw Leah and the family waiting for her near the luggage area in Austin. Leah and Eugen had two sons, Arnold and Simon. Leah's fifteen-year old daughter, Sheana, considered Eugen her father. He had accepted her and considered her his daughter. The void left by the loss of their youngest son seven years ago remained. Emilia was close to all of the family. She had been there when all of the grandchildren were born and had helped as much as she could. Yenta, Leah's twin sister, by contrast had brought her children up to be closer to her husband's parents. Emilia realized that her decision to put Yenta on her own at sixteen had created these reactions. At the time, there seemed to be no other way to resolve the problem that faced her. She was startled by Eugen's voice as he greeted her.

"Mom, it's good to see you," he said, giving her a hug.

Emilia felt the love in the hearts of the children and their parents. For the next seven days, she forgot about worrying about her husband and enjoyed her daughter's family. She had a comfortable bed, and there were no drugs around. People were happy and occasionally sulky also. Leah was working at a job that she enjoyed, although it could have been considered a dead-end job by some. Leah felt positively about her co-worker. This seemed a good omen, Emilia though, thankful to see the absence of depression in her eyes and voice.

Eugen was a good cook. Emilia had the opportunity to sample his cooking, as well as watch him work through 'the voices' when they told him what to do. Like many schizophrenics, Eugen spent a lot of time rocking back and forth and trying to hold the voices in. The medication that he was taking was doing a good job of controlling his problems, and for the most part, he was pleasant and jovial. When 'the voices' began to take over, there was no living with him. This apartment had a patio that allowed him to go out and sit alone without bothering anyone or being bothered by anyone when he needed to be alone.

The children were all in school. The boys were in an elementary school and Sheana was a freshman at the local high school. She had trouble with Algebra and Spanish, two classes that Emilia had done well in when she was in high school. They talked a lot about Algebra, and Emilia who had taken college algebra eighteen months earlier, tried to remember some of the calculations. One problem that they did incorrectly was simply because Emilia hadn't added correctly. It was nice to feel as though people enjoyed having you around.

Leah and Emilia visited the Modern Art Museum and the library on the University of Texas campus. Leah told her that she wanted to go there and take landscaping. It would be a long time before she had the funds to do that. This year, Sheana had to begin applying for scholarships in colleges that she wanted to attend. All of the gifts were placed in the closet in Emilia's room until Christmas. Sheana helped her wrap them. Kitty, the family cat spent a great deal of his time rocking the Christmas tree, and devastating some of the wrapping paper. Emilia used her watercolours to entertain the boys on several occasions. When she got ready to leave, she found that she still didn't have enough room. She had left a lot of the things that she'd gotten in New Orleans at Leah's, as well as some clothes that she had brought from Connecticut. All in all, the visit was one of the best that Emilia had ever had with Leah and her family. The only seizures that she had were in the bright sunlight or in Wal-Mart under their strobe lights. Even these were momentary. She had never considered strobe lights to be a cause of seizures, although other people in her support group considered them problematic.

Sheana and Leah dropped her off at the airport, expecting to spend some time with her. However, Emilia was whisked away immediately and caught an early flight back to Connecticut before Leah had parked the car. Sheana had to hug her and say goodbye for them all.

Chapter XXII

Emilia returns to Connecticut

On her return, Emilia saw Nicole and George near the baggage turn-style where her luggage was coming off. George was sitting down. His body was bent more than it had been thirteen days earlier, and he was using a cane. When Nicole brought her over to where he was sitting, she realized that he had become much worse while she was gone. His head was still cocked to the side, and his body was even more contorted than it had been when she left.

"Mother, it's good to have you home! We missed you." Nicole said, hugging her.

"Where is Moona?"

"She's at Tessa's tonight. I didn't have room to bring both of them, Dad and pick you up."

"Need a larger car?"

"I wish."

"You never know. It would be nice to be able to ride and not feel like you were on the road," Emilia commented.

"Who's this?" George said.

"It's Emilia, your wife."

"Oh Emilia, when did you come in? Nicole's been taking good care of me," George said. "I have to use the cane. They wanted me to use the walker, but I won't do that."

"We'll see." Accepting George's slobbery kiss, Emilia smiled at the man who had fathered her three daughters. He looked older than his seventy-four year and his shaking had increased markedly. Well, he would be seventy-five in six days. She wondered if he had fallen while she was gone. He was leaning heavily on Nicole, and shaking more than previously. Even so, he decided that he wanted to pull her bag. It took both of them to convince him that he should let them do the carrying. Emilia's large bag was easily pulled; but the coats and sweaters caused her difficulty. They walked a bit before they found the car. It had begun to snow, and tonight wasn't the best night to fly into Hartford. On the way home, George talked constantly. Nicole was quiet, and Emilia wanted desperately to go to sleep. It was a relief to be almost home.

It seemed that George had fallen into the bathtub on one occasion. His ribs looked bruised. He hadn't been able to walk the dog as much as he wanted to, and Nicole had taken over that duty. However, he had certainly shopped before Emilia returned. There was plenty of food in the house. They had shopped at the new Wal-Mart store, as well as Adams in West Haven. Emilia couldn't understand his compulsion for buying food. She found canned goods in the drawers where screwdrivers were kept, as well as in all of the shelves above the refrigerator and the counter which held the microwave.

When Emilia had been in New Orleans, she talked with a doctor from Philadelphia who taught students about people who had difficulty breathing. He told her that if George continued to 'aspirate' or slobber from his nose and mouth and have trouble swallowing because of the narrowing opening in the trachea he could die. The increased aspiration coupled with the difficulty in swallowing put him at risk. The trachea could become smaller because of the disease. He advised her to seek help from a Parkinson Support Program as soon as possible. She resolved to contact the support group at Saint Raphael's soon. As they drove down the dark road, she grappled with the certainty that trouble lay ahead.

When they got home, Emilia found the house was clean. Pepper was excited to see her, and jumped all over her. She was too tired to argue with him. After she had had an opportunity to take a bath, and unpack a little, she went to bed. George still slept on the couch. There was a strange smell in the house, but she didn't care. She was home.

Chapter XXIII

George falls

When she woke up the next day, George was walking around the house. He had walked with the cane that night. She had been too tired to hear him. He had been glad to see her and had tried unsuccessfully to have intercourse with her. He gave up, because his body just wouldn't allow it. Emilia knew that he felt badly about the situation. She realized that she needed help taking care of him. So, the next day, she took out the walker from the closet where he had stowed it, and showed him how to use it again. He tried, but he had difficulty holding onto it. His hands didn't have the grip that was needed.

Nicole came over later, and they went for a drive. Later, Moona and Tessa came by after school. The following morning they would be there at 6:00 sharp. Nicole dropped them off there when she had to go to work early. Christmas was coming, and the tree had to be put up. Emilia kept putting off getting the things from the basement. Finally, a week before Christmas, she brought all of the boxes up from the basement. She had gone into New Haven that day and done her final shopping. When she got home, George was asleep on the couch. She left the boxes by the piano, and quietly painted and watched TV. He didn't stir. Then he fell off the couch. George didn't wake, and Emilia left him alone, reasoning that he needed the sleep. He hadn't slept through the night since she'd been home. She covered him with a light blanket and went to bed.

At four o'clock in the morning, she heard him calling her. She got up and found him nude on the rug in front of the couch. He didn't seem to know what had happened. She dragged him into the bathroom, and put him in the tub. She placed his feet in the tub, and when he had settled down into the water, she bathed him and washed his hair. Although she didn't do as good a job as she would have liked, she got him clean. He smelled better. Urine saturated all of the clothes and body. It seemed obvious that he had very little control of his bladder; the situation had gotten worse since she had left. Getting out of the bathtub was difficult.

"Bring that bag over here, and I can push myself up with it." George said, indicating an overnight case by the sink.

"I'll try anything to get you out," Emilia replied.

"This bath felt good. Thanks."

"It's nothing."

So, they worked together to get him onto Emilia's overnight case. Her father had bought it for her when she was eighteen and left for college. George somehow was extricated from the tub, rubbed dry, and dressed. Emilia never figured out how they did it. George's body was like dead weight. He seemed to have lost the ability to move his legs and his arms were all he had to propel himself around.

After he was re-dressed, she picked up the living room couch, and helped him sit back down there. It seemed to be safe enough. By that time, it was six o'clock and time for her medicine, as well as George's. Emilia took hers and George took his. Then she fixed him some coffee and cereal. She probably should have served it in the living room, but instead, she helped him back to the table.

"You sure have provided us with plenty of food, George." Emilia said. "I see that you have gotten plenty of fruit."

"I thought that you'd like that," he said.

Emilia looked at him and noticed that his body was listing to the right side. She hoped that he wouldn't fall out of the chair. They sat there and talked, and then he fell out of the chair. She pulled him back in once. Two hours later, he fell out again. This time, there were workers outside. She went out and asked them to help her get him back in the chair. Luke, who was painting the gutters, lifted him in as if he were a feather. Emilia and George thanked them and continued to talk at the table. A visiting nurse was supposed to come over that day and outline a program for George's home care. Then he fell again. This time, George crawled around the table, trying to hold onto anything that would allow him to get up.

He seemed to have the ability to move both his arms and legs. This time, he got himself stuck among the claw feet of the table. George tried in vain, to get his leg untangled. The more that he tried, the more entangled he became. Rather than continue to pull up on the table, George gave up and asked Emilia to pull him from under the table. The claw feet of the table had a firm hold on George's body. To get him extricated they had to work together. First Emilia moved his right leg off of the claw foot, and it dropped to the floor. Once that was done, she sat in a kneeling position, pulled both legs, backed up, and pulled again and again until she finally got him out. Suddenly, she realized that her left and right hips were sore. Emilia had broken her hip in 1961, and had had five surgeries on it, and one surgery on her right knee. She wasn't in the best condition to do heavy lifting. When she picked George up this last time, she vowed it would be the last.

The new blue jeans Leah had purchased for Emilia last week were perfect for working with George this morning. They allowed her to move around easily on her knees. Yet, they protected her from the bite of the rug.

By the time that George had gotten back into the chair, Emilia decided that she'd push it closer to the table. She also tied him down. Then she fixed lunch. They were just finishing when the doorbell rang. She went to answer it, telling George to hold onto the table.

Emilia saw a smiling blond woman through the doorway. Opening the door, she asked: "Can I help you?"

"I'm looking for George Blake. The insurance company sent me over to assess his health. I'm Jody Pascal."

"Oh, you couldn't have come at a better time. I'm Emilia Blake, George's wife. George is having a bad day and so am I." Emilia replied. "Come with me up these stairs and to the right."

"This is a quiet area of town."

"Yes. I like it." Emilia replied.

Opening the door, Emilia continued, "Let me take your coat. Go on into the dining room. George has fallen five times since yesterday afternoon, and I am worn out. Won't you join us at the table? We are having lunch."

Turning to George, Jody said, "I'm Jody Pascal, George. I came to see if we can get you and your wife some assistance."

"Oh that would certainly help. I keep falling," George said.

"How have you managed to get back up?"

"The first time, my daughter and granddaughter picked me up off of the floor and put me back on the couch. My body tilts to the right and I just go over," George said.

"That's unusual even for Parkinson's disease. We can get you some assistance, but you will need to fill out these forms. First though, let's talk about what you want."

"I want to be able to get some help here at home," George said. "Emilia isn't always here, and even when she is, it is difficult."

"I would need someone at least six hours a day," Emilia said. Even as she spoke, she wondered if that would be enough.

"We can have someone here six hours, but that is about it. If you get full coverage with our plan, that would entitle you to that much assistance. But what will you do the rest of the time?"

"I don't know." Emilia said.

"Do you have trouble eating, George?"

"Sometimes," he said.

"What do you mean?"

"Well, since I started this new medication, I can't hold my silverware or my cup very well. I shake all of the time. It makes me feel like a bag of bones." George said, affecting a smile.

Emilia smiled at him. He was trying to make a joke, she knew.

"Well, we don't want you to think of yourself as a bag of bones, George. We want to help you as best we can." Turning to Emilia, who was playing with her food, she said, "You go ahead and finish your lunch. I can wait, if you like."

"Thanks."

Emilia fed George the rest of his soup, and then ate hers. She asked Jody if she would like some tea or coffee, and was assured that she would like tea.

"I want you to promise me, Emilia, that you will not try lifting George again." Jody said. "Call 911 and you will get help."

"OK. I promise." Emilia said.

Three hours later, Jody Pascal left. She had all of the paper work that she needed, and had explained to George and Emilia what the procedure would be to get home care. Emilia felt that things would get better. They stayed in the dining room for the most part; George used the walker if he needed to go to the bathroom. He did a little better. It had helped to have the nurse visit and reassure them that they hadn't been forgotten.

About five, George wanted supper. Emilia went to the kitchen to cook something different. He had bought about twenty microwaves meals. He told her which one he wanted for supper and she put it in to cook. While George had been living alone in Minneapolis he used these microwave meals, as well as different soups that she had never tried. George insisted that this gave them better-rounded meals in less time. Emilia thought that it was just less trouble.

She heard a fall. When she returned, he was lying on the floor again. "What did you try to do?" She asked.

"I had to go to the bathroom. I didn't want to bother you."

"Well now I am going to call 911." Emilia said with a wry grin.

While she dialed, George just lay on the floor and shook. Pepper, who had been avoiding him today, came over to check on him.

"We need assistance at 155 Clay Street in New Haven, CT. My husband has fallen for the sixth time . . . . No, he doesn't need to go to the hospital." Emilia said.

When the paramedics got there, they found a different chair with arms and placed George into it. Then they tied him securely. The chair that he had been falling out of didn't have arms. But he had been using it ever since he got to Connecticut. Apparently, something was wrong with his balance. "Why don't you let us take your husband to the hospital now?"

"I'd rather have supper first. The last time we went to an ER, we didn't get home till two in the morning. If I am going to go, I'm eating first."

"OK. Suit yourself, but we will be back," one man said.

"Oh yes, we will be back. I can't blame you for wanting to eat first though," said the second man. "Don't let him out of this chair. If he has to go to the toilet, use a urinal

"Thanks for your help," Emilia said.

"You don't need to be lifting him. It looks to me as though you have problems of your own."

"Yeah, I broke my hip in 1961, and I have had my share of problems." Emilia said.

"Well, call if you need us again. Don't try to lift him."

"OK, I'll do that." Emilia said as she showed the paramedics out.

After they had left, Emilia and George had supper. "I don't know why I didn't think of using that Captain's chair," Emilia said. "It's comfortable and it's harder to fall out of."

"It was your Mother's," George said.

"So?"

"I never liked it."

"Oh. How is your supper?"

"Good."

"I called the VA Hospital earlier. They don't have any openings. You'd just get to the ER and stay there. Tonight we'll go to Saint Raphael's Hospital in New Haven. They have a good program for Parkinson's disease and when I called the VA Hospital, I got that same person who just allowed you to stay overnight. He would do the same thing again," Emilia said.

"Good. I didn't care for him."

"Well, when you get through eating, try putting your shoes on."

"I can't do it. You'll have to help me."

"Well, after we eat, I will."

They finished their meals. Emilia cleared the table and then washed the dishes. Afterwards, she got George's shoes out, and loosened the laces. Then she loosened the towels that the paramedics had used to secure George. He managed to get them on, although his feet were extremely swollen. She went to the kitchen to get some more tea. Suddenly, she heard him fall again. This time, he had tried to walk with his cane. George couldn't move his right side. She called 911 again, and asked the paramedics to come back. Then she called her neighbor Grace and told her that they would be going to Saint Raphael's now. If anything happened, they could be reached there. Grace, who was a retired nurse, lived on the other side of the hall on the second floor.

When they got to the hospital, it was eight o'clock. This time they took George onto a wheelchair-like carrier. Emilia rode with the lady paramedic to the hospital. It was 3:42 in the morning when Nicole picked her up and brought her home. Emilia had planned ahead and brought water and fruit, as well as her medicine. Experience with ER's was proving helpful.

When they first arrived, she had to sign George in. The person who talked with her had seen her new book. Another worker told her that they had been told to read it. Both of them commented on the cover and asked Emilia if she had done the art. This was unusually good news to Emilia, whose recent book dealt with abuse and epilepsy. Finally, all of the paper work was done, and she rejoined her husband in the room that he had been assigned. The Emergency Room at Saint Raphael's took better care of their patients than the VA did. Tonight, of course, George couldn't walk. That required the doctor to send him for new X-rays and a PET scan as well. Although the X-rays didn't indicate a break, the doctor wasn't about to send him home without knowing why he couldn't walk.

"We're going to find out why you can't walk, Mr. Blake. We won't send you home until we do," Dr. Mackey said about midnight. "We're busy, but not too busy to find out what the problem is. Just bear with us."

"I appreciate that," George said.

He had been put into a 'Johnny coat' that tied in the back when he first arrived. A light cover had been placed over him. Tonight, he didn't take it off. He lay there and slept, for the most part. He was on his back, and the nurses were constantly re-arranging his pillows to be sure that he was comfortable. The curve in his back made it necessary to have his body lying at an angle, in order to be comfortable.

Emilia sat quietly and read, while George was sent off to have six or seven tests done. She felt that these people were much better than the last two episodes with the VA hospital. She saw no point in disturbing Nicole until she knew that George would be admitted. The assistant nurse practitioner had assured her that they would not be turned away, but she had no idea when their testing would be concluded. When they finally did decide to admit him, it was three in the morning. There were no phones allowed in the ER. Emilia asked if she could call out. One of the staff lent her a cell phone to use.

"Nicole?"

"Mother, what time is it? It is still night."

"It's about three-thirty in the morning."

"Has something happened to Dad?"

"Yes. He may have broken his hip. We're still at the ER at Saint Raphael's. We've been here since eight o'clock last night."

"What happened?"

"He fell and hurt himself the last time. I called 911 twice. The second time, they brought him to the Saint Raphael's hospital. I called the VA earlier, but the same person that we got last time was on. I told him that we were going to Saint Raphael's instead. It's been a long night. There was no reason to call you until I knew what was wrong."

"What are they saying is wrong, now?"

"They think that he may have broken his hip. But the X-rays don't show that it is broken. I know from experience that that can mean absolutely nothing. He'll be here for a while. Can you pick me up? I really would like to get home soon." Emilia said.

"As soon as I finish dressing, I'm on my way. I'm glad that you went to Saint Ray's instead of the VA. Those people don't seem to really care about their patients."

"That's what we thought, too."

"At least here, he'll find out what is really wrong."

"Yes."

"OK, I'll be there soon."

It was a relief for Emilia to have Nicole living in New Haven and able to help her with transportation. She felt a little guilty because she didn't give her daughter money for transportation. But she figured that it all evened out. The orderly was getting George's things onto a cart to take to 4 north where he would be moved.

"Here, Mrs. Blake, take your husband's wallet, and other valuables. I don't want anything to happen to them." The nurse was saying, as she walked back into the room. "We're moving him up to 4—North now. You can check back with the nurses' station there to find out how he is doing later today."

"Thank you, I'll do that," Emilia replied, as she saw Nicole enter the room. "At least George will get some help."

"Yes he will. His leg doesn't look broken, I wonder why he can't walk?"

"I don't know. My bet is that the X-ray is wrong, and it's fractured," Emilia said.

"You might be right," the nurse's assistant said.

"Good. Good. You take your mother home now. I'll see you all later." George said as he was being wheeled out the door.

"Well, let's go," Emilia said, as she dressed for the December weather.

"Why didn't you call earlier?"

"Why not let you sleep? You couldn't do anything here. I got a ride with the medic to the hospital, so there was no need to bother you. Where's Moona?"

"Asleep."

"That figures."

"I just couldn't handle the VA Emergency Room people again. This is much better. Why, they even like my new book." Emilia said.

"Did you sell any Mary Kay?" Nicole laughed.

"No. I didn't try. The nurses were helpful, and they took a lot of tests. More than they did at the VA. But, of course, tonight he couldn't walk. That apparently makes a difference. We'll return later this evening and find out what they finally decide to do."

"OK. I work the evening shift today, so I'll check on my way to work."

"At least, you are close enough to do that." Emilia said. Nicole worked as a nurses' assistant at Yale New-Haven Hospital.

When they got home, Pepper was going manic. Nicole took him out after she had fed him. Emilia was too tired to do anything but get to bed. "I'll see you in the morning, Mother." Nicole called from the kitchen.

"OK. Thanks again."

"No problem."

Chapter XXIV

George has hip surgery at Saint Raphael's

Later that day, Emilia was called by the operating physician to verbally give her permission for George to have surgery on his hip. Apparently, they had found a hairline fracture in his right femur bone.

Emilia knew from experience how difficult this fracture is to properly diagnose. However, George's bones were so brittle that the doctor on call believed that there might be difficulty setting the bone. Surgery was scheduled for the following day.

Emilia believed that they should wait until after surgery to see George, but Nicole had wanted to visit him right away. Dr. Moore hadn't told her which room he was in. George didn't have a phone and was asleep when she called the nurses' station, so she talked to the nurse in charge. The nurse told her that he had been asking for his daughter, Leah. At first, she was surprised by the request, but then she remembered that George had always treated Leah special. Leah was the only daughter who had stood up to her father. Apparently George had respected her. Emilia requested that both Leah and Nicole should be advised of their father's condition if they called. If something happened to him, they would be notified immediately. She didn't want what had happened in Texas to her to happen to her daughters. When her father had died, she was unable to find out how or why from the hospital. Emilia had no desire to return to the hospital that she had left only six hours earlier. But she assured the nurse that they would be by that evening.

That night, George looked like a ghost. He was lying quietly on the bed. His face looked gaunt and tired. The stubble of a mustache was beginning to poke out of his face. Nicole, Moona and Emilia entered the room. George was alone. Nicole sat down. Moona and Emilia talked to George. He said that he liked the hospital better than the VA, but his hip sure hurt. When Emilia saw Nicole bury her head in her hands, as she had done as a child when faced with a difficult take, she knew that her daughter needed her. She left Moona talking to George, and went over to hug Nicole.

"You've got to be strong for your Dad," she said. "What's wrong?"

"He reminds me of some of the patients that I have at work. He looks so helpless. I never believed that I would see my father looking this helpless, but he does. There's nothing that I can do to help him. It's so frustrating."

"Nonsense, you can smile and talk to him. Look what Moona is doing. She has him talking to her," Emilia said.

"I guess you're right Mom," she agreed. "Can we call Leah when we get home? I need to talk to her."

"That's a good idea. I don't have Yenta's phone number, or I'd call her too," Emilia replied.

George seemed to be getting tired, so Nicole walked over to the bed and kissed him. "Dad, we're going now. You'll feel better after the surgery tomorrow," she said.

"Yeah, I guess so."

"Sure you will," Emilia said.

As they walked out, Emilia was very aware that George hadn't had much to say to her. She wasn't surprised, but it did hurt a little. She told herself that she should have expected it. Still, it did matter.

Chapter XXV

Hip surgery I and II

The surgery took place on the twentieth. The following day was George's 75th birthday. Emilia suggested that this year they buy his birthday cake, not make it. He had been transferred to the Orthopedic floor, 5 West. When they came in from the hospital garage, they took the same route, but when they got to the elevator, Moona hit 5. In this room, he was nearer the window, rather than being by the door. It gave them a little more privacy, but not much. Before he hadn't had anyone in the room with him; now he shared the room with another man who actually looked in better shape.

George had a small piece of birthday cake, and Emilia and the girls had some too. Then they gave the rest to the nurses in charge. Since it was close to Christmas, there were a lot of sweets being left for them. The nurses thanked them and assured them that it would be eaten. They would make sure that he got some more tomorrow if he wanted it.

Emilia was glad that she had chosen Saint Raphael's Hospital. Her mother and another friend had both died here, but she herself had had excellent care in the ER on two occasions. Once the doctor had changed the strength of her anticonvulsant; the other time, they had given her pain medication for her hip. She'd always considered it one of the better hospitals in New Haven, even if Nicole worked at the other.

After the surgery, George's legs were enclosed by a machine that vibrated them constantly. It was supposed to keep blood clots from forming in patients who had to lie on their backs for long periods of time. The machine was also supposed to lesson the shooting pains that he had had when he came into the hospital. At any rate, his feet began to be less swollen and he seemed more able to lie on his back. When the machine was removed, on the twenty-third, he again turned on his left side and resumed the fetal position that he had slept in before he came into the hospital. Sometimes when they visited, he didn't seem to make much sense when he was talking. On the day after Christmas, he told Moona that he was planting a garden and demonstrated how he was shoveling. Nicole was so upset that she left the room. Moona and Emilia kept talking to him and feeding him his dessert. Periodically, George would reach out for Emilia.

From time to time, he would ask when Leah was coming to see him. Then he would return to talking about planting his garden. Emilia wasn't certain whether the anesthetics that he had been given during the operation had left him this way or if it was simply the disease progressing more rapidly. The nurses were interested in keeping him from moving, but they didn't have a great deal of success after the machine was removed. George seemed to twist around, even if he were in pain. Mona, the evening nurse, described him as a very good patient. Yet, Emilia worried that he was no longer aware of the present. After the 26th, Nicole had difficulty visiting, stating that he reminded her of some of the terminal patients on her floor. George's insurance was covering his stay in the hospital, but the social worker had told her that she would probably have to change his insurance once he was placed in a nursing home. On the 28th of December, George would be transferred to Silver Valley Nursing Home in Milford. He had been excited about going there. He still talked about the Veteran's Home in Rocky Hill that Emilia had insisted that they consider. He didn't realize that the only program that interested her was respite care, which was free. They charged as much or more than the nursing home in Milford. When George arrived at Silver Valley Nursing Home, the physical therapist sent him back to the hospital, claiming that his hip was re-fractured and turned in-wards.

This proved to be true. Apparently, George's bones were so brittle, that the hip had broken when he was dressing to leave. Surgery was scheduled for the following day. Emilia was called and talked at length with Dr. Daikstra, Dr. Moore's partner. The surgery that he described sounded much more durable than the previous surgery. Since George's bones were very brittle, the doctor planned to put a metal rod into the hip, and tighten it with four screws. This would be done lower than the previous surgery and would hold the hip in place in a more durable manner. Emilia had had similar hip-surgeries herself, and she knew that it would work. Dr. Daikstra asked her whether or not George could be trusted not to put weight on his foot. She didn't think that he could, and said as much. So, when he was transferred back to the nursing home, it was mid January before the doctor considered physical therapy.

The second operation had gone more smoothly than the first. The doctor was happy with the surgery. He explained everything to Emilia and told her to call him if there were questions. In order to keep George from taking off his covers, the nurses at the Nursing home placed a call button on the arm of his 'Johnny coat;' so when he moved to take off the covers, they came immediately.

When Emilia had gone to the Nursing home in late December, to fill out the paperwork, she had talked at length with the administrator and been very satisfied with the place. Nicole and Emilia had difficulty finding the place originally; but afterwards, they had little trouble at all. The Social Worker at Silver Valley told Emilia to apply for Title XIX, a government program that assisted in paying the nursing home bills for some senior citizens who qualified. Emilia had considered this before, but had not acted on it. This time, she was relieved to find that the person that she was dealing with was honest and forthright. She had to provide a lot of personal paperwork of her and her husband's finances when applying for the program. Emilia still attended the Epilepsy Foundation Support Group in Milford, and was relieved when at the February meeting; the speaker discussed Title XIX at length. Even in March, she was still hearing about how long it took to get things accomplished with this program. George was considered a terminal patient who would remain there until he died. It was May before he was accepted. Emilia was assured that Title XIX would back-pay the five preceding months.

Section VII:

January 2005

Chapter XXVI

Emilia takes George to the Orthopedist;
she grows ill

The second week in January Emilia was asked to accompany George to the Bone Specialist's Office. It was cold. The temperature was supposed to drop to 20 degrees that night, too cold for more snow. Emilia took a bus over, and then met the Amerivan Driver at the nursing home. George was whisked out of the home with only a thin blanket over him. Emilia, who had on about five layers of sweaters and coats, was concerned about George. The driver had a little difficulty finding the building, but when he did, he dropped them off. George was in a wheel-chair with which Emilia wasn't familiar. She wished that an attendant from the nursing home had accompanied them.

"I have to go to the bathroom," George said.

"What do you want me to do about it?" Emilia replied.

"Take me there."

"I'll see if I can find a urinal first." Emilia said. She went to the secretary and asked for one.

"We don't have one," replied the secretary.

"OK. Well, where is the rest-room?"

"It's over there."

Emilia saw no alternative but to wheel George into the men's restroom. She got him in and asked, "Can you unzip yourself and go?"

"No. Guess I'll have to do the best I can." George said. "Get me out of here."

At this point Emilia, who had no experience pushing wheelchairs, hadn't expected to have the responsibility dumped in her lap. She had trouble with the chair, the doors, and of course couldn't lift George so that he could relieve himself. She was more upset than George or the doctor realized. A half-hour later, they were seen. Emilia had wanted to accompany George in order to talk with the doctor. He wanted her there to answer some of the questions that he had. Although the doctor seemed quite understanding, Emilia realized that it was getting later than she had anticipated and tabled some of her questions.

After he was seen, George was told not to weight bear on his leg until the doctor told him to. He wanted to make certain that the bone had healed completely before George did that. Emilia had the secretary call the Amerivan to pick them up. It was five in the evening before the driver arrived. The weather grew colder as the sun had set. This time, the van driver didn't have a seat for her. He finally found a small chair. When they got back to the nursing home, she paid him, and then went in long enough to deliver the paperwork from the doctor. Then Emilia walked to the center of town to catch the last bus. It was thirty minutes before the J4 bus arrived. She was freezing. That night, the bus dropped her in the center of New Haven, rather than taking her all the way home. She had time to eat supper on the Green, and then she waited another thirty minutes for the bus to take her home. If it had been warmer, she might have walked. But tonight it was near twenty degrees and a fierce wind was blowing. Huddling into the protective covering of the bus stop, Emilia shivered and ate, shivered and ate. When she finally got home, she could not get warm. Her nose was stopped up, and she knew that she would be ill. In the middle of the night, she felt fever creeping over her body. She took an aspirin, and drank hot tea with lemon juice and honey. This was the remedy that her grandmother had always used, and that she had used with her own children. By three in the morning, she realized that she couldn't talk. She'd had two aspirins, twice, as well as four cups of tea with honey and lemon juice. She got more covers on the bed and burrowed down into them. Still, she was cold. Emilia could hear the wind blowing outside the corner of the building, making her bedroom even colder than it ordinarily was.

The following morning, she called Nicole's apartment and talked to Moona. She could barely hear her own voice.

"Oh, Gigi, you have the flu."

"Yes, I guess I do," Emilia said.

"I can barely hear you. You sound sick."

"I am sick. Now tell Nicole to get me some cough syrup."

Late that night, Nicole arrived and slammed down a bottle of Nyquil on the table. "That's all I have, and I don't have any money or time to get anymore," she fumed.

Emilia didn't even want to ask what was wrong. She could barely talk as it was. A day or so later, Nicole called to see how she was and explained that that night she had had a migraine headache and felt terrible. She eventually got Emilia some Robitussin, but by then, Emilia was too sick to care. Later, she figured that the flu had turned into pneumonia, and it was just lucky that she had taken as much tea, honey, lemon juice and aspirin as she had. The Nyquil did nothing at all for her, except give her a sweet taste in her mouth. She was sick for sixteen days. And for that length of time, all she did was sleep and drink honey, tea and lemon juice. She ate some soup, but she stayed in bed. Reba called her to check on her, and so did her friend Jana. Then, about half way through the illness, she got a call from a man in California who wanted to help her get a new mortgage. He was pleasant and his terms were good. She had been approached by about ten other people the week before, but this person had a good deal, and she could see saving $150-200 a month on the cost of the mortgage, as well as lowering the interest rate by 3% as a good thing. So, although she felt terrible, they managed to work out a good deal. The rest of the time, she slept. Pepper wasn't taken out unless Nicole happened by. He made a mess, but was forgiven.

During the second week, she woke up from a dream in which she felt as though she had been to heaven and returned. After the dream, she looked in George's telephone box and to her surprise she found a copy of a letter that she had written him two years earlier in which she had talked about marriage being a mistake. He had claimed that he never received it. After reading it, she realized that he had used her to get someone to take care of him. He had known that the Parkinson's disease would get worse, and he had wanted her to take care of him. She'd fallen for it. Emilia became angry. She knew that George didn't really love her. He just used her. She had fallen in love with him again in October because she wanted to be needed, but now she realized that she didn't want to be power driven. It drained her life, even though this time she had the power, not George.

Reba was relieved to know that she had finally figured this out. Emilia told her the words of a song that had always been in her mind, but now made sense.

I do believe the Lord above
Created you for me to love,
He picked you out from all the rest,
Because he knew I loved you best.

If I get to Heaven, and you're not there,
I'll write your name on a golden stair.
If you're not there by Judgment Day,
I know you've gone the other way.

I'll give the angels back their wings,
their Golden Harps and all those things.
And just to prove my love is true,
I'll go to Hell to be with you. Be with you.

These were the words of a Hawaiian song that Emilia had learned years ago. Jane Kekahuna had taught it to her, and Jane, who was pure Hawaiian, had told her that if George continued to hit her, life would only get worse. And it had. "I feel free," she said to Reba. "I know that I don't have to wait for George when I get to Heaven."

"That's right. You don't," Reba said. "See, things work out for a reason. You had to help him out in order to set yourself free."

"Yeah, I think you have a point."

"Go back to sleep, Emilia." Reba said. "I'll call you tomorrow."

"OK," Emilia replied. She knew that she didn't want to leave the bed. And stay in bed she did. Her throat began to feel a little better, but her voice still sounded like a frog's.

Chapter XXVII

Emilia paints while she is ill

After George had entered the hospital in December Emilia became gradually aware that the couch in the living room had to be replaced. The indentation and odor that George had left were embedded into the furniture. One day, she saw an advertisement from Hitchcock Furniture in Orange, and phoned to see if their sale was still on. After stating the reason for her call, Emilia added that she sold Mary Kay Cosmetics, as well as books and art. Julie, the saleswoman asked immediately if she had a yellow concealer."

"Yes, I do. I can bring it to you when I come out to look for a new couch. Would next Saturday work?"

"Great. I'm sure we can find a couch that you will like," Julie replied. "I have been looking for a new consultant."

"I'll see you on Saturday." Emilia smiled to herself at the prospect of a new couch and a new customer.

When Nicole drove her out the following Saturday, she sat on several couches. She found a couch which didn't fold out into a bed, and was very comfortable. She and George had always had couches that folded out in case company stayed over. The present couch had springs that were shot, thanks to a pre-teen's over exuberance, and a hamster's chewing. This would be Emilia's choice. Julie told her that it would be two months before the couch was upholstered in the material that Emilia selected. This gave Emilia time to paint new pictures to hang above the couch.

The second week that Emilia was ill, she felt well enough to paint from time to time. Expressing herself in watercolours had always relaxed her; but now she had a reason to paint. She began painting the pictures that she wanted to hang behind it. They were of Chinese Dragons fighting one another and were on the back of the tea canister she had recently bought. She painted with her left hand, went slowly and they came out just as she had anticipated. The couch would be covered in an apple green material, and the Dragons were that same color. They would be matted in Dark Forrest Green and placed in gold frames. Emilia knew exactly how she wanted them to look. The pictures that she had hanging on the wall now had been done in the 1980's in Minnesota. They were good, and the frames were unusual, but she needed something more current.

The pictures took her two days to complete. Emilia drew them in ink with her left hand, and then painted them. She had found that when she drew with her left hand, she took more precautions, and often did better work. She believed that they would accent the couch. That week, she painted constantly. She had plenty of paper, and paints. At times, it was as though the Spirit moved her hand. Some of the pictures were different from anything that she had painted before; others were similar, but better. Emilia tried various techniques and paints to accomplish the end result that she wished with each picture. Because painting allowed Emilia to bare her soul to the world, it was important to her to take the time to do it well. If she were to go back to school, she feared that she might not have the time to paint and to write as she felt she must.

Reba had been excited about the new pictures. She liked Emilia's work, and from time to time had purchased certain pictures. In fact, she had some of the pictures Emilia considered to be her best. Yet she was quick to tell her friend when Emilia's work wasn't up to par.

Nicole and Moona visited from time to time. When they were there, Pepper got to go outside. Otherwise, he stayed in the house.

When she felt better, she called the nursing home and discussed the necessity of having someone else go with George to his appointments. This would allow them to be able to monitor his condition and take him to restrooms if necessary. She also made another appointment with the social worker who handled Title XIX or Medicaid.

It was late January before Emilia ventured out of the house. The weather was still unseasonably cold, and snow continued to fall. Nicole took her shopping, because she was running out of food. They also went to Orange that day to pay for the couch.

Section VIII:
February 2005

Chapter XXVIII

George's will and his will power

Emilia had talked to Patrick about the necessity of George having a will. He had never made one, and the paperwork that he had was from Minnesota. Patrick felt that the will should be drawn up in Connecticut, since that was now his place of residence. The girls had been after him for years to make a will, but he had put it off. Now, since he was not well, and Emilia had no idea how long he would live, it made sense to have it done.

"Emilia, you do realize that people in a nursing home cannot be participants in a will, don't you?"

"No. It never occurred to me that they couldn't. What are you saying, Patrick?"

"You need to let me draw up George's will, then arrange for a time when I can come out with witnesses and a Notary Public to execute the will."

"That sounds reasonable. Send me a copy of the will, and I will leave it with the social worker at Silver Valley. Then she can contact you about a time that would be convenient for all. Would that work?"

"Sounds great, I'll get right on it." Patrick said. "How are you feeling, Emilia?"

"Aside from having a terrible bout with the flu or pneumonia, I'm OK. My seizures are under better control than they were last month. George still upsets me and that sets off my seizures. Your uncle knew that and it was one reason that he wanted me to leave George in the 1970's. Our families have known each other a long time. I first met your dad in 1954. Mother knew your Grandmother. It helps to have friends, Patrick."

"Yes it does. Is George still having hallucinations?"

"Well, if you consider his actions the day after Christmas, I would have to say yes. It's difficult to know whether the drugs for pain or Parkinson's disease enticed him to act as though he didn't know where he was. That day, he kept trying to get out of bed to plant a garden in the hospital room."

"You have a lot on your plate, Emilia. I wish you the best of luck," Patrick said, as he rose and ushered her out of his office. "Don't hesitate to call if you believe that I can help in any way."

"How are your children?"

"Great."

Smiling, Emilia put on her coat and left. She glanced up at the picture of Daniel and could have sworn that he winked at her.

* * *

When he was between operations, George had had problems with his urine. He had pulled out the tubing that was used to collect it, and had had to have minor surgery to repair his damage. Now, George had another Foley placed to collect urine. He wasn't at all satisfied with that. When Emilia visited, he couldn't get out of bed. He told her in no uncertain terms that she needed to start planning for their trip to Milwaukee. George had been looking forward to the Navy Reunion, and several of his friends had called to ask how he was. He was determined to go.

"Emilia, it's getting close to that time when you need to start planning for our trip."

"What?"

"The trip to Milwaukee, I'm going. The doctor says I'll be able to walk by May."

"It's only February, George. You have to consider your needs. Besides, your credit card company won't allow me to use your card. How do you propose to pay for it?"

"You can do that for me."

"No, I can't. You have to consider everything George. Who is going to drive you from the airport? Who is going to dress you? I can't. I have told you that time and again. I can't lift you. I know that it means a lot to you to go to this reunion, but you are going to need to pay for yourself, an attendant, and me to stay at the hotel with us. That costs money. Money we don't have."

"My Navy buddies will dress me. You'll see. All we need to do is get there. The hotel will provide the transportation there."

"Do you know how to use your wheelchair to get about?"

"By May, I will be an expert, or I'll be walking," George said.

"OK, but you will have to make the reservations. If you want to call the credit card company, I'll leave the information here. When Nicole comes over next week, you can borrow her phone and call them."

"Put it in that drawer over by the bed." George said.

"Mother, I don't think you should do that." Nicole said. "Who knows who else would look at his information, I just don't think that it is wise."

"Well, you have a point."

"Dad, why don't I just bring the material over and let you call them next week?" Nicole said. "Would that be OK?"

"Yeah, that would be better. We'll do that." George said. "Could you bring me a chocolate bar with almonds too?"

"Sure."

They were about to leave, when the housekeeper came in. "Mrs. Blake, we have lost your husband's clothes again. Is there any way that you can get him some new ones?"

"This is the second time that you have lost them. The first time, you said that they were put with the sheets and towels. What's going on?" Emilia asked.

"Well, I just don't know. He goes through so many pairs of slacks that he is constantly running out. They are talking about putting him in diapers soon. My suggestion would be to buy some new ones, mark them good with a marker, and then when they get dirty, take them home and wash them."

"I can do that," Nicole said. "I came in here the other day and he was dressed all in pink. I know that Dad doesn't like to be dressed in pink. Mother, why don't we go shopping today, and then I'll bring the clothes over after I have them marked. Is that alright?"

"Nicole, that's a good idea. It would help out a lot. I can't do it. You are the one with the transportation. When we leave today, we'll get you some new clothes, George. How is that?"

"Great. Don't forget the chocolate bars."

Nicole leaned over and smiled at her Dad as she kissed him. "I won't."

Emilia kissed him good-by also, and they left. When they were back in the car, Emilia asked her where she wanted to shop.

"Wal-Mart, we'll go to Wal-Mart in Hamden. Moona is going to be upset because the nursing home lost the shirt that she got him for Christmas. I know I would be."

"Yes, she probably is." Emilia said. "I never did take all of his clothes over to the nursing home. So, we do have some things at the house. Most of the shirts that I still have are short sleeved, though. He's probably lucky to still have his coat and one pair of shoes."

"Oh, he doesn't have any shoes. The ones that he wore to the hospital were lost."

"I didn't know that. It's a good thing that they gave me all of his identification and his watch when we checked in. You know that the last time I visited your Father here he gave me his wedding ring to hold on to. He claimed that he was afraid it would slide off and get lost. I have to confess that that hurt my feelings a little. But, nowadays you never can tell about people."

Nicole drove down the highway and tried to concentrate on the road. In December, Emilia had helped her get the money from George for the down payment on the new car she was driving. It drove like a charm. Everyone fit into it. They had found it the week after Christmas. George still didn't know that he had helped her out. Nicole wanted him to have his own clothes. Yet, she wondered what it would be like to do her father's laundry on a consistent basis.

"How about we stop at Burger King and get something to eat on the way?" she said.

"OK."

They drove to Hamden, stopping on the way to get some nourishment, and ate in the car as they continued on to Wal-Mart. When they arrived, they picked through clothes until they were satisfied with a medley of 6 shirts, and five pairs of slacks, socks, and tee shirts. Emilia, who had been made George's Power of Attorney in November to handle his finances, signed the check for the clothes, and they left. On the way back, Nicole stopped at the house and got five handkerchiefs that George had requested.

"I think that we did pretty well," Emilia said. "He should like these shirts and slacks. I hope that they don't lose them again. They probably will though, with my luck."

"They better not. I want Dad to have his own clothes."

"It's really great of you to mark them and wash them for him." Emilia said. "I certainly appreciate it."

"I'll get Moona to help me. It won't be a problem." Nicole said. "I'll leave you at home, and then go do the marking. Can we call Leah?"

"Sure. Is he still asking for her?"

"Yeah, he dreamed about her the other night. He thought that she was visiting him in the room."

"That's wild. Since I was sick so much in January, I really appreciate your looking in on your Dad."

"Well, when he had that pink outfit on, I figured something had to give." Nicole said. "They weren't his clothes and he looked like a girl."

Emilia smiled at her daughter. Once they were inside, Emilia called Leah and handed the phone to Nicole. The two sisters talked non-stop for thirty minutes. Nicole had to tell her about George losing his clothes and Leah had to relate what was going on with the kids and Eugen. It wasn't easy living with a man who had schizophrenia. She enjoyed talking to her mother and her sister. While Emilia had been ill, she'd called three times. Yenta still hadn't called, and her phone number had been changed. Rudy, George's son had been written a long letter, and had called back once to see what was going on in December. But for the most part, it was Nicole and Leah who kept in touch. George's sister-in-law, Francis had been called before Thanksgiving when the hallucinations had begun. Francis was head of the nursing homes in South Dakota and she knew a lot of answers to Emilia's questions. Emilia had also written his youngest brother and his sister. They wrote back and asked how George was. Emilia saw no reason to write his sister until she had all of the facts. And she still didn't have all of the facts. She knew that his hip was healing nicely from two surgeries, and that he had some problems with cognition. He had Parkinson's disease and was unable to hold his urine. But why keep going over that? So, she just wrote to his friends and family and gave them the bare information. It seemed best.

Section IX:

March 2005

Chapter XXIX

Emilia approaches the social worker about the reunion, Nicole and George talk about Alex

Emilia felt badly that she couldn't do what George wanted. It was a good thing that he was excited about getting well enough to go to the reunion, unrealistic though it might be. She needed someone to talk to about the fact that he was determined to attend the reunion. She called Kelly, the social worker.

"Hi, Kelly, I wonder if you could help me."

"Sure, Mrs. Blake, if I can. What's up?"

"Mr. Blake seems determined to go to *'the Navy Reunion'* in Milwaukee in May. To me, it seems impossible. I can't handle him by myself, and I would need someone else to go with us. Could you talk with him and see if you can persuade him to give up on it? Or would that be a bad idea?

"Oh, I think that it is an excellent idea to find out what he really intends to do. I'll stop by tomorrow and talk to him about it. He can't seriously be considering leaving the home and going by plane to a reunion, can he?"

"That's what it sounds like to me. I just don't believe that he is considering what it will involve, or that he will probably lose his bed at this nursing home. The main thing seems to be *'The Navy Reunion'*. Whatever you can do will be appreciated."

"I'll talk with him tomorrow. I think that we can resolve the problem."

"I really appreciate it," Emilia said.

Kelly put her phone down also and wondered what George Blake could possibly be thinking. He was still getting over two surgeries on his right hip; he wasn't that ambulatory in the wheelchair yet; plus, Parkinson's disease was doing a serenade on his muscles. It left them weaker and more tremulous than before. One of the medications that he took aggravated this as well. "No way can Mr. Blake go to Wisconsin!" she said aloud to no one in particular.

"What did you just say?" asked Ellen, the other social worker.

"Oh, I have a patient who wants to go to Wisconsin in May. I can't see him doing it. I wasn't really talking to anyone."

"George Blake? Yeah, I heard him telling his wife that she better get the tickets this week, or else."

"Or else what," Kelly asked.

"He didn't say. Frankly, Mrs. Blake didn't seem that excited about going."

"I don't think that she is. He's nice, but sometimes he gets belligerent when he doesn't get his way," Kelly said. "I told her that I'd talk to him tomorrow."

"You do that," Ellen said, as she left the room.

* * *

The following day, Kelly wandered up to George's room. She found him sitting in his wheel chair, watching the other people in the room. He was still in his 'Johnny coat' and hadn't been dressed. One of the housekeepers was making the bed.

"Hello, Mr. Blake."

"Hi, Kelly, what are you doing today?"

"Oh, not much, I wanted to talk to you. Is now a good time?"

"Good as any, I'm not going anywhere and it will be a bit before anyone dresses me. They can't find my clothes. I hope that they don't give me those pink pants again." George said.

"Your wife told me that you are planning to go to a reunion in May. Is that right?"

"No, I wish that I could. I have resigned myself to the fact that I can't go. I wanted Emilia to meet all of my friends, but it looks as though she won't have the opportunity."

"Well, we wouldn't want to have you leave until you're well enough." Kelly said.

"Did she ask you to talk to me?"

"Yes."

"She believes that I am going," George said. "I can't figure out why."

Kelly smiled and remembered another man who had lived there. He was always upsetting his wife with tales like this one. It allowed him to remain in control of her life. She could see that Emilia Blake was planning to take back control of her own life.

"I don't know, Mr. Blake. It's hard to figure people sometimes. I'll stop by the nurses' station and see if we can't find you some clothes to wear that aren't pink. Is your daughter supposed to bring your clothes back today?"

"Yes she is. I even have her bringing me two candy bars, chocolate with almonds."

"You're lucky to have such a nice daughter. I'll see you later," Kelly said as she left the room. She decided to call Mrs. Blake back and let her know that George wasn't going anywhere. She stopped by the nurses' station and asked why Mr. Blake wasn't dressed.

"No clothes."

"Well, find him something that isn't pink to put on." Kelly said.

"OK. Look here's his daughter now. She's got plenty of clothes."

Nicole was dragging the two bags of clothes down the hall from the stairwell. The elevator had taken too long and she had decided to use the stairs. Now she asked herself what had ever possessed her to do that. When she got to her Dad's room, she dropped the bags. "Here are your clothes. What would you like?" she said.

"Oh, I don't know maybe a green shirt and pants? Do you have those today?" George said with a smile. "I'm not Irish, but I feel like wearing green."

"Well, they're in here somewhere," Nicole said.

"Nicole. Sit down for a while and talk to me. Can you stay for a bit?"

"Yes. I can stay a little while. I don't have to be at work for three hours."

"Well, I wanted to talk to you about your mother."

"What about her? She's feeling better."

"Did you know that she told me that her father had a son?"

"What? That can't be right. She was an only child. Mae was adopted a year before I was born."

"She thought that she was an only child. Alex had a bastard child. She told me in December."

"Well, she didn't tell me. If he did, I'm sure there is an explanation. I won't believe it until she tells me and I see proof. Grandpa wouldn't do something like that. Did mother use the word 'bastard'?"

"No. I used it. Your mother probably doesn't even know what it means." George said.

Oh, she knows what it means, Nicole thought. You don't give her enough credit, and you like to hurt her. Aloud she said, "Well, whatever. I've got to go now. See you." And she was out of the room without giving her Dad his usual kiss. She left the chocolate bars on the bed table.

On the way down the stairs, she never stopped. She was angry with her father for putting her grandfather down. He couldn't be right, she thought. She got into the car and drove to the house. When she got there, her mother was cleaning the living room floor.

"You've been to see your father?" she asked.

"Yes, and do you know what he said?"

"No."

"He said that Grandpa had a son."

"I told him that in confidence. I should never have trusted him to keep his mouth shut. Yes, as far as I know I do have a brother. However, until I talk with him, I would prefer not to mention it."

"I don't believe it," Nicole said as Pepper jumped into her lap.

"Well, I've been looking into the matter. I've found some information that sounds good. It could have happened," Emilia said. "You know, Nicole none of us is perfect."

"Yes, but Grandpa?"

"Can't he be allowed to make mistakes?"

"I guess so."

"That's better. Dad was only a man." Emilia said. "Not God."

About that time, the phone rang, and Emilia answered it.

"Hello, Kelly. Yes. Oh, that's good. Thanks for telling me. Bye."

"What was that all about?"

"George has decided that he can't go to the reunion. I imagine that he was using it to get to me. Well, this is one time he didn't succeed," Emilia said with a smile.

"That's a relief. I have to get going. I need to take the car in for a lube job before work." Nicole said. "Thanks for listening, Mother."

"It's no problem. Just don't worry about what your Dad says. I'll let you know if there is any truth in the matter."

"OK. You know I don't believe I'll visit Dad for a week. I'll get Moona to drop off the clothes. I don't want to listen to him gossip about Grandpa," Nicole said as she went out the door.

Emilia shook her head as her daughter left. She wondered why George had said the things that he had. She remembered that Leah was always telling her, "Dad likes to gossip, Mama. Don't you know that?" She thought about calling Leah, but decided to wait. Of all the girls, Leah probably understood her father the best. She was the only one who had had therapy so that she could tell him what she thought of him. It had taken her close to three months of intensive therapy, but she had done it. Nicole and Yenta had written George, but never confronted him about the way that he had treated them. The Domestic Abuse Project in Minneapolis had contended that if people didn't confront their fears, they wouldn't be able to live with them. There was some truth to that. Emilia had had her own demons to face. Sometimes she felt guilty because she had remained with George so long before she divorced him. There had been no way that she could do otherwise, though. As an epileptic with a broken hip, she had never had much success getting jobs even before she met and married George. After they married, he had made her quit working for the Marines to stay at home, although they had no children at the time. She often wondered if leaving George in the 1970's would have made any difference in their lives. Emilia knew that she hadn't been able to because he had had a hold upon her that she couldn't break. Even their divorce hadn't set her free from George's presence in her life. She had been unable to break loose from him until he was in Silver Valley Nursing home, and no longer able to overpower her psychologically. It was sad that even when they had remarried last October, he hadn't been honest with her. Maybe, Nicole was right. Maybe George had just married her so that he would have someone to take to the Navy Reunion. It was evident that he would do what he could to make her feel guilty about his condition. Why else would he have made such a to-do about going to the Navy Reunion when he knew that it was impossible? "If he thinks he can control me, he has another think coming," she said aloud.

When she had told Reba what Nicole believed, Reba hadn't been surprised. "He doesn't know how to love, Emilia. He never has." Reba's words reverberated in her mind as she continued to clean the floor of the living room on her hands and knees. Pepper had really done a number on the floor. It seemed as though he was messing more and more in the house.

"I guess George spoiled him last fall. He took him for long walks. I don't. The dog likes to get out early in the morning. I have to admit that I don't," she said to herself.

When she reached the piano bench, she looked at it closely. Until recently, she had had magazines piled upon it. Last month, she'd put them away. "What is this?" Emilia said. "It looks like the bench is falling apart again." In November, when George had taken it completely apart, she had believed that he had succeeded in gluing it back together completely, after he had 'removed all of the termites' that he told her were in it. The piano had been her grandmother's and was a special style that had only been made for only five years. Although she had not believed that there were termites, he had the bench apart before she knew that he was going to do so. At the time, she had been glad that he had found something to occupy his time. Now, she had wondered if he had damaged it beyond repair. "I guess I'll have to have this fixed. For now, I'll reverse it so it doesn't look so bad," Emilia murmured.

Chapter XXX

George begins to look worse, has his medicine changed, and takes less interest in Emilia

Neither Emilia nor Nicole visited George the next week. Moona dropped off his clean clothes, and picked up the dirty ones. Nicole continued to give her father some space. She washed his clothes each week, and sent them back with her daughter. Finally, a week after Valentine's Day, she asked Emilia if she wanted to visit George.

"Not really. But I suppose I should," Emilia answered.

"I thought maybe you might like to see him," Nicole said.

"Remember in January, I told you that if I kept having seizures when I saw him, I would visit less and less?" Emilia asked. "Well that has happened. I really don't want to visit and feel as though he is continuing to use me."

"Well, do what you tell us to do. Face him and tell him what you think."

"I thought I had already done that. Remember that we got into a fight over buying the tickets to Milwaukee?" Emilia replied. "Then he tells Kelly that he really didn't plan to go. I should tell him off again. But why upset myself?"

"Maybe you're right. I'm just asking."

"No, I'm glad that you are. I need to see him, just to prove to myself that he isn't getting to me any more."

"So, shall we go?"

"Yes. Wait till I change my shoes. Oh, what shift are you working tomorrow?"

"Why?"

"I'm going to Boston to visit Reba."
"I should get off at three in the afternoon."
"Pick me up at the train station?"
"Sure."

They drove back to Silver Valley Nursing home and visited with George for a while. Later, they went to the market Nicole had found that specialized in fresh fruit, Asian tea, and fish. Emilia liked it, although she rarely had enough cash to get what she wanted. Today, she bought six kiwis for a dollar. You couldn't really beat that price.

"Have you heard anything from the publishing company lately?" Nicole asked.

"No. Not since they sent me a blurb about publishing a second book."

"What about the royalties?"

"Not yet," Emilia replied. "You know that writing never has brought in a lot of money. I get satisfaction from knowing that hopefully my readers are learning something about the topic that I write about," Emilia said. "That's my main reward. In the case of the last book, I hope that they enjoyed my art as well."

"I started reading the book last week, and another nurse wanted to buy it."

"Did you sell your copy?"

"Yes."

"Well, then I guess you need another copy to show around."

"That would be good. Mother, what are we going to do about Easter this year? I will be working Easter Day. What about Easter Dinner."

"Well, why don't we have it at my house after your shift ends?" Emilia said. "I can cook the ham that I have, and you guys can bring whatever you want to eat. Will that work?"

"Yeah."

* * *

The following day, Emilia caught the early bus to the train station. She wanted to go to Boston on the 9:15 so that she would have enough time to visit. Reba had some things to tell her about their project, and had suggested lunch at *La Fonda's*, a good Mexican restaurant near the station. After Reba moved her business to Cambridge in 2003, Emilia rarely saw her daughters-in-law and grandchildren as she had before. She missed them.

The trip up was tiring because none of the signals was working and everything moved very slowly. When she had visited Reba in February, they had had lunch and then gone shopping. Today they had lunch at *La Fonda's* and enjoyed the food and conversation. After lunch, Reba had to do other things, and Emilia went back to the train station and painted while she waited for the 4:45 train. It began to grow colder. Although it was the last day of March, and spring had technically begun, the weather felt more like winter. Emilia had brought enough clothes; they were packed in her case. She finished two pictures while she waited. One was of a Greek scarf that her friend, Duke had talked about the previous evening; the other was an interpretive piece that she liked. Lately Emilia had been painting on rougher paper than she was today, and she had found that it took washes better than the slick paper. Emilia took her time, and finished without any problems.

She was relieved to get on the train and leave the city. She and Reba had had a great visit, and she hoped the return trip would not be as slow as the trip to Boston. To her relief, the train made its usual fast trip. The signal lights had been fixed. She made friends with a research physician from China who worked in Children's Hospital. The lady was intrigued when Emilia told her that she had been in Beijing in 2002 for a medical conference. Her acquaintance showed her pictures of her two daughters, Hanna and Mary. Hanna was eleven years old, and Mary was eighteen months. She got off two stops past Providence, RI. That seemed like a long commute to Emilia, but she figured she would have done the same, if she had had the opportunity.

As they left Providence, Emilia resumed painting. Over the years, she had devised a way to hold paints, water, and paper securely while traveling on trains or planes. Her cell phone rang, and Nicole told her that she had stayed at work and couldn't pick her up. There were still busses running, so Emilia wasn't too concerned. She continued painting and then put her paints away, and closed her eyes. Soon, they would be in New London, and then in New Haven and home. When Emilia arrived in New Haven, it was a little past eight. She had been sitting so long that she wanted to walk. She caught the city bus to the Green immediately, and as it wasn't that cold, decided to walk home. It was about sixteen blocks, and would take less time than waiting for the next bus which came in an hour. At the time, the brisk walk was enjoyable.

Emilia had decided that in March, she would look into two graduate programs in New Haven, one on Public Health and the other on Art

Therapy. She understood what Public Health would allow her to do, but she had received several different accounts of Art Therapy. In Minnesota, she had wanted to take the program on weekends in a crash course, but George, who would have had to drive her there, had vetoed the program, immediately. Emilia wanted to make a difference to other people. Ivan Lesný and William Fields, two noted neurologists respectively of Prague, Czechoslovakia and Houston, Texas had been instrumental in making her aware that she had talents which could be used in the medical field. Because of her seizures, she had ruled out medicine, and society had ruled out special education in the 1950's. Emilia felt that if she could write and paint in a way that would teach people about epilepsy, she might make a difference. Over the past twenty years, she had investigated material on other topics, namely cerebral palsy, Friedreich's ataxia, bipolar disorder, and genetics as it relates to hidden disorders. Her son-in-law wanted her to write about schizophrenia, but she hadn't tackled that yet. It would come in time. Nowadays, people had to have credentials to make money doing anything, it seemed. Emilia liked education, but she'd had so much trouble in the past, that she anticipated trouble in the future. That was the reason that she hadn't gone into Art Education. When she had left the counselor at the Art Therapy program, she realized that the program offered in New Haven was counseling and that wasn't what she wanted.

Earlier in the week, Duke, a friend she had known for two years, called to ask if she could pick him up from the hospital. He was going in for same day surgery. Nicole agreed to pick him up and after Emilia returned from the university, they picked him up from the hospital and took him home. He was an interesting person. He had Asperser's syndrome, a neurological disorder that Emilia had had to look up in her Medical dictionary. It affects speech, hearing and balance in a multiplicity of ways. They talked for a while that night and Duke appreciated the friendship that she and Nicole extended.

Chapter XXXI
Easter 2005

Easter had come and gone without George really seeming to notice it. He was intent on the fact that Leah should visit him, and always told Nicole to make sure that she used good maps. George didn't seem concerned that Yenta hadn't come for Easter. Emilia wondered if he really knew that Sunday was Easter. He acted as though one day was the same as the next. As long as there was food, he was happy. Leah had phoned Emilia twice, only to get the answering machine; so she was relieved when her mother called to see how she was.

"I don't know how we'll be able to get to Connecticut." Leah said. "Ramsey County is keeping my tax returns. I figured it would happen eventually. I make just enough to pay my bills. Since Eugen doesn't work, even though he gets SSI and SSDI it is hard."

"Well, what if your Dad and I put aside $300 for the next three months, and then added a little, would $1,000.00 be enough?"

"Yeah, that should do it. I really want to see Dad. You know I'm the only one of us girls who had counseling to talk to our Dad. I don't think Nicole and Yenta ever have been able to stand up to him. He respects me because I did."

"You may have a point. At any rate, *you have to visit George and soon*." Emilia stressed. "It's hard to say what we can expect."

"Yeah, I know. I was reading about Pope John Paul II today. He had Parkinson's disease like Dad does. Once his organs started going, a lot of things happened fast; same way with Daniel."

"Yeah, you're right. Your uncle Conda had it too."

"He's the one who used to call us 'his little rainbows', isn't he?" Leah asked. "I never met him, but I always liked his letters and phone calls. Didn't he have a bunch of cats too?"

"Yeah, when he moved up to Arkadelphia from Houston to be near his daughter, he did have cats. He was a good man, and his wife Beanie was a jewel." Emilia said. She remembered how much love the two of them had given her when she was growing up. They had always had kind words for her mother, Malia, as well. One thing about the Granger family, they didn't shirk on loving their 'kin', as uncle Conda would have said.

"Call me back next week, or I'll call you. I love you, Mother."

"I love you too. Have you heard from Yenta and Theo?"

"No. I don't expect to."

"They didn't get here for Easter, of course. But at least, I suppose they are all right. I'll write her when things get rough with your Dad. I've written her once, and I've written your brother once. He called back, and his wife wrote. That's about it."

"I've got to get ready for work. Bye Mother."

"Bye. I love you."

"Love you too."

Chapter XXXII

Silver Valley Nursing Home and Insurance

Since George had entered the nursing home, Emilia found herself playing Black Jack with the insurance companies. The first company had lasted a month, and then she had had to change to a different company in order to make Medicare George's primary insurer. In February, she had also found another company that would act as his secondary insurer. The prior month, she had filed Title XIX for assistance from the state. Four months later they were still waiting on approval. For a country that was supposed to have life, liberty and the pursuit of happiness at its forefront, America's insurance system didn't even meet the needs of the individuals who couldn't afford insurance. Emilia wondered at times if socialized medicine would be any better. She decided to give the state two more weeks before complaining again. One had to stay on their tail, but Emilia believed that one couldn't stay too close.

George was being given physical therapy again. His broken hip had finally healed. If only he could control his urine, he might be getting better. Emilia was well aware that Parkinson's could go slowly for a long time and then proceed very quickly. It wasn't an easy disease for the patient's family. George's conversations were better at times than others. Some days were better than others. He no longer dreamed of their daughter Leah. That's what her sister-in-law, Francis had told her to expect. She hadn't talked to Francis since December. Francis didn't call Emilia to check in on George. Nobody in the Blake family did. Sometimes when she was lonely, it was a relief to have Reba and Jana to talk to. Reba was in Boston; but she knew that Emilia needed someone to talk with about George. Jana kept her out of the doldrums because she understood what Emilia had gone through the first time that she was married to George, and she didn't see much hope for improvement. Salma, another friend who knew George, kept her opinions to herself, but she was there for Emilia. Emilia found that having her own business was a positive thing. It kept her mind on other things. When she had been married to George the first time, she had been totally dependent on him. Now the situation was reversed. Emilia had an opportunity to get her life back together. Emilia believed that friendship, respect, and trust were important elements in living a good life. These elements had been lacking in any relationship that she and George had undertaken. When they remarried she had believed that he was her friend, and did respect and trust her. Now, she knew that that was 'hogwash.' He'd just acted as though he did to entice her to go along with his desires. She had good male friends who respected and trusted her. George wasn't among them. He preferred to keep her on a leash. Now that he couldn't, he wasn't that interested in her.

Emilia wondered if she would have to divorce George in order to get Title XIX to go into action. It might be necessary. When she had married him, she had lost her alimony. If she divorced him again, the question of who would be designated as his Power of Attorney would have to be addressed. Everything happened for a reason, she surmised. Whatever it was, she hoped that her life would change; for Emilia believed that she was falling into a whirling bottomless pool. She knew however, that it would be up to her to keep an open attitude about life in order to enjoy what cards she was dealt.

* * *

The card that was dealt next was CANCER. Emilia had a mammogram in April, and that had led to a biopsy of her right breast. The thought of having cancer was something that she had considered carefully over the years. Her mother had died of the disease, as had her maternal grandfather. Even Leah had had cancer. The radiologist, who discovered the possibility of cancer, asked her to begin looking for a surgeon immediately.

"Mrs. Blake, you'll need to find a surgeon to do the surgery, once we have done the biopsy."

"Oh, that shouldn't be a problem. Dr. Kaffka always finds me a good specialist," Emilia replied.

"Aren't you concerned?"

"Sure, but we have to find out what is wrong and rectify the situation," Emilia replied.

"I wish other people had that positive an attitude," the radiologist replied.

"When do you want to schedule the biopsy, next week?"

"Sure, is Tuesday alright?"

"Yes."

Emilia left Temple Medical Building and immediately called one of her good friends, Jana. There was no point in telling Nicole that she had cancer, she would go to pieces, and Emilia didn't want to have to take care of her."

"Jana, Emilia here. Are you free to pick me up at Temple Medical building next Tuesday about noon?"

"What's this?"

"Oh, I have to have a biopsy and I can't handle Nicole right now. Would you mind?"

"Of course not. How will you get there?"

"On the bus," Emilia replied.

"OK. Are you still going to the meeting tonight?"

"Sure. Can you pick me up?"

"Yes, about 6:00?"

"Fine, see you then."

Placing her phone back into her purse, Emilia walked a block to the bus stop and realized that graduate school would have to be put on a back burner for a while.

* * *

On the day of the biopsy, Jana picked her up as scheduled. They were both a little quiet because it seemed that Emilia did need to have surgery and that had already been scheduled for the following week. Jana agreed to pick her up from that also. It would be done at Yale. When the day finally arrived, Emilia couldn't reach Jana, so she had her daughter paged. Nicole worked on the sixth floor of the hospital. Luckily, they both arrived together. Nicole was in tears.

"Take a deep breath, Nicole and ask your mother, 'How do you feel, Mother,'" Jana said as she held Nicole's hand.

"How do you feel, Mother?" Nicole asked.

"I'm fine, ready to go home." Emilia said. "The surgery went very well."

"Why didn't you tell me?" Nicole asked.

"Because I knew that you would be upset, and I didn't want to deal with it," Emilia replied. "I suppose since you are here, you can take me home if Jana doesn't mind."

"That is not a problem," Jana said.

"Good. I should have had your cell phone number, I suppose."

"Nicole can handle this now. Let me know if you need anything further."

"Thanks. I will."

So saying, Jana walked out of the recovery room, and Nicole assisted her mother in getting dressed. Emilia was surprised to see how efficient Nicole was. She had talked to Leah and told her of the impending surgery, but she hadn't told Yenta or Nicole. Nicole had been talking the week before as though she would die if anything happened to her mother, hence her decision to have the surgery and then tell her daughter.

At the end of May, Title XIX was officially in place. It would be another two months before the payments would begin. Emilia found herself looking at a co-payment of $1912.50 for the first six months, and then in July, the payments would be $2150.50. George was only allowed to keep $57.00 of his income for haircuts and travel as Title XIX is a part of the welfare program, Medicaid. Emilia wondered just where the money for his laundry would come from. Nicole had been washing his clothes regularly since the second time that the nursing home lost his clothes. Much of the time there were dirty clothes in the wash that didn't belong to George.

On June 2^{nd,} a second surgery was scheduled for Emilia to make certain that all of the cancerous cells had been removed. It went very easily and reassured Emilia that she wouldn't have cancer again. The cells that had been removed had been non-invasive and prevented the cancer from spreading to other parts of the body. Emilia needed only to rest as she had done before. The surgeon's stitches were very small. Dr. Pond scheduled Emilia for five weeks of Radiation Therapy beginning in July. She felt extremely lucky that Chemotherapy hadn't been needed. One of her acquaintances was having a terrible time with similar surgery because she had needed Chemo and radiation as well. Her cancer had been discovered in December, and for some reason, it had taken her a longer time to get through the process than Emilia. Emilia was thankful that it had gone so quickly.

Leah and her family arrived in early June for a visit. Everyone enjoyed himself or herself and George was delighted to see them. He perked up and seemed to act as though he felt better. Emilia wasn't that interested in how he felt. The doctor was telling her that she had to have radiation therapy as soon as possible. That would be late June or July. She hadn't bothered to inform the nursing home of her problems, because she didn't feel that they'd be that helpful. While Leah was there, she did talk to her attorney about a possible divorce or annulment of her marriage. She was still waiting to hear from him. It would probably be the end of the summer before she could put this marriage behind her and turn the Power of Attorney over to Nicole, as she was the oldest child living in the area.

Much of the time, Emilia found that she was too tired to really function. Her business had been going down hill, but in May, she had decided that she would fill out the requirements for becoming a star consultant with Mary Kay, Inc. and she did. She felt better when she talked to new people and got new customers interested in the products and the business. By the end of June, she was recovering nicely from the surgery and yet she still didn't have much energy. She spent a great deal of time painting, reading or watching TV. The purchases that she had made came and were filed away in the cabinet that contained her products. Then she made a list of all of her customers in an endeavor to assess her clientele. She discovered that she had more customers than she had believed and called them all.

While Leah was there, she spent two days cleaning her house. She got it spic and span in no time. Emilia doubted it would stay clean for long. Pepper did try harder not to mess in the house, now that it was clean, but he only partially succeeded. Leah, Eugen and the boys went back to Texas on the 18th of June, but Sheana remained until early July to visit with Nicole and Moona.

During May and June, Emilia had noticed an increase in her seizures. She attributed this to the humid weather and the infection that had accompanied the Cancer. The stress created by having house guests coupled with the need to pay off the nursing home was also a factor. She set about finding a way to pay them the $10,400 that they demanded. It wasn't until the end of July that she succeeded.

She put more of her time into painting because it relaxed her. She enjoyed her granddaughters, but didn't see them that much. Moona graduated from Middle school on June 21st. Nicole and Sheana drove Emilia to the graduation. Sheana would be in the tenth grade in the fall. Moona was only nine months younger, but she had been held back in the first grade to improve her reading skills. Now, she had become a good reader.

Before Leah left, she insisted that Nicole and Emilia find another nursing home that would take better care of George. She noticed little things that Emilia and Nicole had overlooked. Emilia realized that George wasn't happy at the place. It had been the only nursing home available in late December. Six months later, it was evident that it was difficult for Nicole and Emilia to visit often, and other things that Leah noticed made her question the advisability of leaving him there.

Nicole got a list of nursing homes before Sheana left and Emilia called them. They finally settled on a nursing home that was five blocks from Nicole's home, and easily accessible. It had larger corridors, more rooms and more activities planned for the patients. They both realized that they had been there before. In September of 1979, they had walked from here to the center of New Haven, a total of 40 blocks, after having supper with Malia, Emilia's mother. For the past ten years, they had been trying to find it.

"If they could handle Grandma, they can handle Dad," Nicole said.

"I agree. I also know that she wouldn't have been placed in a home that wasn't caring," Emilia said.

It would be a while before George could be transferred there. But he was excited at the prospect of being nearer to them. Leah and Yenta believed that their father would be in a better facility than Silver Valley Nursing Home.

* * *

The following week, Emilia began her radiation treatments. The treatments themselves took only a few minutes. But it took a while for Emilia to catch the bus over there and back. The first two weeks went easily. However, the third week, she had more seizures and grew increasingly tired. The fourth week she had a seizure every day; yet the last week, she had fewer, although she continued to grow more tired. The doctors didn't seem to know much about the effect radiation had on epilepsy. They knew what effect it had on people with diabetes, but then there had been more available research on diabetes. Emilia's reaction was predictable. More research needed to be done. But she didn't know who would do it.

"There's no question that the body fights infections by having more seizures. It probably doesn't know whether or not the infection has left, since the radiation is still going on." She said to Dr. Wong, the oncologist.

"You have a good point. It could be that your tension is increasing more than you realize. Also, you are tired out from the treatment and that could increase your seizures also, couldn't it?"

"True."

"Did you go off the osteoporosis medication as I insisted?"

"Not completely," Emilia replied. "I'm afraid that my bones will grow worse."

"Remember my telling you that Evista was fooled by the cancer once. It may allow you to develop cancer in the other breast. You can't take any chances, Emilia." The doctor said as he leaned back in his chair.

"OK. I'll go off it now."

"Good. I'll want to see you back four weeks after our last appointment that is about September 9th, OK?"

"Sounds good," Emilia said as she stood up. She hadn't been allowed to wear brassieres since the surgery and she felt as though she were only half dressed.

Chapter XXXIII

August 2005

Relief flooded Emilia when the last week of Radiation Therapy had ended. She had had to hang her pictures and those of her mother's in the City Library that week. She and Nicole had done it. She asked friends to come and look at them on the 18th of August when she had a reception at the library. Nicole had taken her shopping two days before and they had purchased what she needed. They had forgotten paper cups, plates, and napkins. Nicole was tired and didn't want to stay out late, so they shopped hurriedly. On the night of the Reception, Nicole called to tell her that she was sick, but would drop her down there. Emilia assured her that that was fine.

Jana had agreed to meet her there and bring the cups, plates and napkins that were lacking. Emilia had packed her valise with books, two tablecloths, and two napkins that they would use. She had a punch bowl, ladle, several trays and the food.

The librarians were very helpful and led them in through the back door when they arrived. Emilia had changed the pictures the week before and included some pictures that she had done in the spring. Although the table was set with care, there probably would not be many people there for the book reading and signing that Emilia planned to do. She was glad to see several men, and two ladies arrive. Jana had come first and helped her set everything up. One of the ladies had three children and during the evening, she talked to them about possibly teaching the middle child to paint in watercolour. The other lady bought a book. The book from which Emilia was reading was about abuse, and parts of it were difficult for her to relive. She blacked out momentarily while she was reading, but apparently, no one seemed to be bothered. One man was interested in discussing epilepsy, so he had an opportunity to see a woman go through a mild seizure and keep going. Emilia realized that she was having trouble reading and gave the book to Jana to read. Jana handed her something to drink as she continued to read. That allowed her a little time to collect herself. All went quite well.

Chapter XXXIV

The Mortgage and the Divorce

Emilia's friend in California finally completed the paperwork for a new mortgage that would allow her to pay off the nursing home, $10,400.00 for the months of January through May. Although, Medicaid had said that it would pay retroactively through January, it hadn't. Instead, Emilia was trapped. It would be mid October before all of George's bills were paid. The amount that the state wanted each month seemed to fluctuate in an upward spiral. Emilia found it difficult to live on her reduced income and still take care of George. Until the end of 2004, she had had about $912 from George that had been a part of her income for sixteen years. That had been the settlement from their first divorce. Emilia continued to hope that the second divorce she was pursuing would lower the amount of income that the state took. It wasn't only the lowering of the income that was important; it was important for Emilia to be her own person and that wasn't possible as long as she and George remained married.

In October, Emilia sent the money to the publisher for her next book. It should come out soon. She finished the 50 pictures that she wanted in the book and took them to the photography company to have them put on disc format. George seemed to feel better. The neurologist had taken him off of gabapentin (Neurontin) which lessened his shaking and improved his alertness although he complained about his legs hurting. It seemed apparent that the disease had a stronger hold on him than he would admit.

In November, Emilia invited some friends over for Thanksgiving dinner. Moona and Nicole cooked most of it, but Emilia did the turkey. It seemed as though she always did the birds.

In December, she went to Washington DC for the American Epilepsy Society conference. It was icy and snowed a lot. After she found a second hotel and transferred there, she had a good time. She even worked on the book while she was there. Traveling didn't provide the pleasure it once had, as she always felt alone. She had many more seizures than she had anticipated having and there didn't seem to be any way to predict when they would occur. These seizures were different because she would lose all consciousness, but most people never detected them. She couldn't talk, and many times if she were standing still, she began to walk without realizing what she was doing. Several times she found herself 8 blocks from where the seizure began. Some days the doctors never even knew that she had complex partial seizures as she avoided talking and had learned long ago to get away from people or sit down when they began.

When Emilia returned home, she remained exhausted. She had ordered a rose bush for George for Christmas. It came, but it was frozen. She nursed it back a bit and gave it to him for Christmas. It died. She wondered if this was an omen. He had told her that he had received the divorce papers in November, but he didn't sign them until Mid-January in an attempt to forestall the divorce, although he had said that he wouldn't fight it.

When they went to the court house so that he could sign the paperwork needed, they waited a very long time. It was cold, and Nicole stayed with them for a while, and then left. It would be late summer of 2006 before the divorce was finalized. They ran into a friend that neither had seen for many years. It was enjoyable chatting with him. Emilia realized that she didn't dislike George; she just knew that she couldn't physically or emotionally handle him.

Finally, Patrick arrived, and he guided Emilia and George to the correct area. He prevailed upon George to sign the paperwork he had been resisting. After talking with a legal counselor, he did so. Emilia called Amerivan to pick him up and take him back to the nursing home. It was cold and windy on the corner where the courthouse was located as Emilia waited alone for the J4. She was exhausted from the time spent with George, yet she was relieved as she waited for the bus which seemed to take forever.

Chapter XXXV

Emilia turns over the Power of Attorney to Nicole; Emilia starts going to SCSU for her masters in Public Health. Reba still asks for money

It took a while to talk Nicole into taking over the Power of Attorney from Emilia, but she knew that her mother was no longer legally able to handle it. Nor was she able to emotionally handle her father's finances. So she agreed. Actually, Nicole was relieved that she hadn't had to take it over in 2004, when George first went into the VA hospital. Nicole doubted whether or not Emilia had considered this when she remarried her father. At least, everything was set up. All she had to do was take care of her father's finances. She promised herself that she would do a better job than Emilia had.

Nicole loved her father, but it was difficult to see him so ill. He seemed to look sallow these days. Nicole wasn't certain that she trusted Patrick. He had sent them to an attorney in northern Connecticut when they first investigated Title XIX, and that person had not helped them at all. Two visits were enough to convince Emilia and Nicole that the attorney didn't really understand their situation. She thought that George had big money. Well, anyone who knew her father knew that he spent his money. He never held onto it.

Nicole thought about what Moona was cooking for supper. She was a good cook. Nicole was enjoying having her cook for them. She rarely cooked and hoped that her daughter would be around for a while. She was a freshman in high school and making good grades. Her height made her look older. Nicole tried to imagine what her daughter would become. Would she be a doctor?

* * *

When Emilia returned home she resumed work on the manuscript she was editing for Dr. Nwangwu. She had met him in 2004. After he had proof-read the revised copy of *Epilepsy a Personal Approach, 2nd Ed*, he had asked her to collaborate on an epidemiology test book. Emilia had agreed if they could include a section about epilepsy and other neurological disorders. She had spent the next few months looking at what was available on the bookshelves for the epidemiology student before looking at the manuscript that he had begun. The following spring she took his introductory class in Epidemiology in order to understand his thinking on the subject and better comprehend what should be written. She took a course in Introductory Statistics as well, reasoning that she would have to understand biostatistics in order to write about them. Next year, she was determined to go into the Masters program in Public Health. Her counselor had expected her to do so it in 2005, but cancer had held her up that year. This fall, it seemed as though cataract surgery might stop her again, but she was determined to complete the work that she was doing on the book before August of 2006.

Emilia was still having problems with Statistics. She believed that she registered for the Epidemiology class as an observer rather than a student. Truth to tell, all she wanted this year was to find out how the professor taught epidemiology and what he considered important. She had tried since 1995 to get into that particular field, but Yale had turned her down flat, stating that she didn't have a high enough GPA. Well, now she did. Emilia tried to overlook the fact that too much of the time she was too tired to concentrate; and that she had to beg for rides home late at night. One way or another, things would work out. After all, she was a survivor.

The winter of 2005-2006, she had spent most of her time transferring the notes that Dr. Nwangwu had given her onto her computer and rewriting some of the Power Point material. She had found information in other books that could be used to reference material from his slides. Emilia had spent a lot of time at the Yale Medical Bookstore, looking for information in public health books that dealt with epilepsy or other neurological disorders and found nothing that dealt with epilepsy. This strengthened her belief that the time was ripe for a textbook that talked about epilepsy and other misunderstood neurological disorders.

* * *

Placing the Power of Attorney with Nicole lifted a heavy burden from Emilia's shoulders. She had enough problems as it was. Reba had called last week to tell her she needed to see her. Emilia knew that Reba wanted to go shopping because 'the spirits' needed to be satisfied. Reba hadn't spoken of her brother in over a year. Could Nicole be right about Reba's true colours? As she rubbed her eyes, she admitted that it was growing more difficult to read. She had begun to use a magnifying glass more than she cared to admit. It seemed that it would take much longer to finish the book. Emilia was hoping to finish her portion by the end of August. Honestly, she was afraid that her eyes would go before then.

Fortunately the statistics teacher had taught her to use the calculator, as well as allowed her to sit in the first row. When she had difficulty reading the board, he would let her go up later and read the formulae there on the board. She learned to like statistics, and began to understand statistical tables in journal articles that she had to read.

* * *

In June, Emilia and Nicole went to visit George. Emilia stayed and talked with him and had lunch in the dining room. Nicole left, because she had to go to work. After Emilia finished eating, she left and caught the bus home. George apparently left as well, but no one noticed.

George turned right, after he came out of the dining room and headed for the doors. He pushed them open, and found himself in a small hall. He could see light through the next set of doors, and he wanted to go out. As he pushed the doors, they opened and he found himself falling in his wheelchair down the steps which were very steep. He grabbed for the railing and held on for dear life.

"Help, Help, I need help!" he screamed for more than 30 minutes. Just as his hands were growing weak, he saw a young man running to help him. Somehow, he was able to get George down the remainder of the steps, and onto the rocky ground. He wheeled him around to the front door and into the Silver Valley Nursing Home.

"What have we here?" the receptionist asked.

"I want help!" George cried.

"Where did you find him?" she asked.

"Hanging onto the back steps for dear life and about to fall out of his wheel chair," the delivery person said. "You should not allow your patients to go out that door. He could have been killed."

"Mr. Blake, why did you go out the door?"

"I wanted to go outside, and I did."

"You opened those heavy doors and went outside?"

"Yes."

"Noone in a wheelchair has ever opened them before." Turning toward the Director's offices, she called, "Mrs. Drake, Kelly get in here now."

"What's wrong? Is Mr. Blake hurt?" Kelly asked, arriving before the Director.

"Mr. Blake went out the back doors. He could have killed himself on those steps. It is a mystery to me that he only has a few scratches."

"Don't you believe you should take him over to the hospital and have him checked out?" the young man who had rescued asked.

"We have our own doctors here. Thank you for saving him."

"No problem. You OK, bud?"

"Yes, I'll be OK now. Thanks for your help," George replied.

"Then I'm off. Glad I could help you." He turned and left, shaking his head in disbelief.

"Let's get you upstairs and in bed and make sure that nothing is wrong. Kelly, call Mrs. Blake and tell her what happened. She likes you. Something like this would make her daughters furious with us. We could be sued." Turning to George, the Director asked, "Don't you wear an ankle bracelet?"

"No, never had one. Should I have one?"

"Mr. Blake, they are called roving anklets. If you had had one on, it would have beeped when you tried to go outside. I'll put one on you now." Kelly said as she wheeled George toward the elevator door and away from the director.

Kelly put the roving anklet on George and settled him in bed. She asked the on-call doctor to check him and make sure that the nurses were aware of the situation. Then she left to call Emilia.

* * *

Emilia was just getting onto the second bus as her cell phone rang. "Hello, Kelly? Is something wrong?"

"No, Mrs. Blake, nothing is wrong now. George went out the back doors, and fell down the steps in the wheelchair. He's alright. Someone heard him calling out and rescued him, and brought him around to the entrance where he must have been trying to go. I just put a roving anklet on him. If he tries this again, it will beep." Kelly said.

"Why wasn't that done earlier? He could have been killed! Let me talk to the director."

Gladys took the phone. "Everything is just fine now, Mrs. Blake. You shouldn't worry about a thing."

"I won't, but Nicole and Leah will be over to talk with you later." Emilia said, ringing off. Next she phoned Nicole at work and told her what had happened. Then she talked to Leah and Yenta. After that, she decided she'd done enough harm to Silver Valley Nursing home and relaxed. "That man has 101 lives." She said to no-one in particular. Pepper looked up at her and nodded his head

Section X:

Summer, 2006

Chapter XXXVI

Emilia is invited to Helsinki by Amir. Her marriage is annulled. She completes the edit on the epidemiology book, has a book returned, and publishes a new book

After classes were over, Emilia considered retaking Statistics, which she had failed. To her surprise, the head of the Math department told her that as she had never paid for the course, they couldn't give her a grade. They understood that she was taking Statistics so that she wouldn't have such a daunting time the following year when she took Biostatistics. She never worried about the epidemiology grade, only recognized the fact that the teacher was satisfied, and they had been able to cover the remaining part of the book that she was editing. That summer, Emilia's latest book came out, and she decided to take it with her when she was invited by a colleague to attend the European Epileptology Congress in Helsinki. She had sent a copy of the book to Milo in Slovenia, as well. He always helped her advertise at medical congresses. The divorce would be finalized in August at last. Just as she was beginning to believe that she wouldn't have enough money to manage, Reba gave her $900.00. Actually, she was supposed to get $1,000.00, but Reba spent $100.00 for food, which was typical for Reba.

"Where have you been?" Emilia asked.

"Away." Reba replied.

"That is obvious. Where have you been?" Emilia asked again. "I needed to talk with you several times this spring and summer, but I could never reach you."

"The work called me out of the state. Then my husband's brother died. I was sick for a while. Oh, Emilia it was terrible. I understand what your seizures are like."

"How could you understand?"

"I had seizures. How can you manage to take them so lightly?" Reba's face showed her concern for her friend. "I never knew that they were so mind boggling."

"Well, I wouldn't consider them mind-boggling, but some of the stronger seizures can really exhaust a person."

"Yes. I found that out."

"You had those?"

"Yes. I had all the types of seizures that you have told me about."

"Why?"

"I wanted to experience them, so I could help you get rid of them." Reba replied. "What's a friend for?"

"I would never ask anyone to go through that." Emilia said softly.

"Well, I did," Reba said. "How are your eyes?"

"I am having difficulty seeing fine print, but I am almost done with the book that I am editing."

"Guess what the spirits told me?"

"I don't know," Emilia answered. She wasn't sure just how much of Reba's story she was buying.

"You're going to meet a new man! Isn't that exciting?"

"When?"

"Soon."

"Anything else?" Emilia replied, falling for Reba's line.

"First you have to have more faith in the spirits. You have stopped believing in the work, Emilia. I can't complete it with you acting this way."

"What way?"

"You aren't burning the candles I told you to. You are listening to your daughters too much. You must remember never to say anything about it to anyone but me."

"You are never around," Emilia replied. "Besides, I am barely making ends meet. This is the first time in years that you have helped out at all."

"Emilia, I am hurt. You forget what I do for you. Night and day, I am working on your behalf." Reba said, twisting her lips into a pout. She was a pretty woman, but she was acting more and more like Malia had acted when she was very drunk, and Emilia wondered if Reba was drunk.

"I have to take care of myself, Reba. It is evident that no-one else will."

"I am thinking of moving to Connecticut."

"Why?" Emilia asked. "Your family is in Boston."

"No, they moved. Shannon is in Medford, and Stacey is still in Cambridge."

"So, why did you want me to come to Boston?"

"I wanted to see you, silly." Reba smiled again.

After having lunch at the Mexican restaurant that they both liked, Emilia got the money from Reba. Then they shopped. Emilia missed the mid-afternoon train as well as the 5 pm train. Because Reba insisted that they go to 8 stores. She waited for three hours at Back Bay Station before she boarded the sleeper which took her home. She was cold from the air-conditioned station, and tired from walking and sitting on concrete slabs. Emilia wondered why she even came up here. She knew the reason. Reba claimed that she was helping her mother, Malia, get to a better place. She also had earlier told her where her brother was, but then she had stopped talking about him completely, as though he was of no interest to her. Emilia wondered what had caused the switch in her attitude. She wished that she could get her silver back from Reba, as well as her Grandfather's clock. Those were two things that she consistently asked for and was denied.

When she arrived in New Haven, it was midnight. She walked home from Union Station, as the busses had quit running completely. It was warm, but not humid. Tonight she wasn't carrying a lot of things, so walking wasn't a problem. Other times, when she had walked home, she had difficulty because of the bags that she was carrying.

* * *

Once she was home, she collapsed on the bed and slept till morning. Pepper, for once didn't bother her. He had been taken out when she got home. It wouldn't be long until she was on her way to Helsinki, Finland. Her bag was practically packed. She was taking three copies of one book and two of the other. She wondered whether she would actually have enough money when she returned to pay the bills that Reba had run up today. Discounting the problem for another day, she smiled and worked on the epidemiology manuscript. Life seemed good.

"Mother where were you yesterday?" Nicole was shouting from the door.

"I went to Boston to get money from Reba." Emilia answered calmly. "Don't you remember my asking you what time you were working yesterday, and you said you were doing a graveyard shift?"

"Oh. Well, Leah and her family will be here in three weeks. She called me last night and we decided that she could move back up here where I can find her a job at the hospital."

"That would be good." Emilia said. "Where are they planning to stay?"

"With you, until they find a place."

"I hope that they can sleep on the floor. That is the reason that I did not get a couch that could fold out." Emilia said. "I'll be glad to see them. Usually they don't last long here before they find a place."

"I am excited. I miss Leah, and Dad is really happy."

"That's good," Emilia said.

"When does your flight leave?"

"It leaves day after tomorrow at 11 a.m. Is that going to be a problem?" Emilia asked.

"No. If we leave here at 7 a.m., there should be no problem. I'll get you there two hours early, as usual."

"That's my girl. I really do appreciate your taking me and picking me up at airports. We had a good time in 1988 when we went to Ireland, didn't we."

Nicole rolled her eyes at the ceiling. "Yes, but it rained a lot."

"True."

"And you got raped."

"I didn't plan to be raped."

"I know." Nicole looked at her mother with a soft look in her eyes. "Do you think you'll take Moona to Africa in 2008?"

"Let's take it one year at a time, one country at a time." Emilia replied. "Besides, you never know what will go down in 2008. I might not even go."

* * *

The following day, she flew out of Bradley International Airport on her way to Helsinki, Finland. Emilia had her watercolours in her purse, as well as a book that she had bought at the airport in Hartford. Why not? She never bought things for herself. As the plane climbed into the blue sky, she looked down at the clouds below. She usually tried to get window seats so that she could take pictures, or draw pictures. Today, she watched the clouds and thought how lucky she had been to be invited by a friend to this conference. Before, she had always gone alone, and come home alone. Well, she would come home alone this time as well, but she needed to find out more about her friend.

Helsinki proved to be an adventure. She had believed that she would remember how to get to the hotel, but after taking a bus into town, she got lost, and had to take a cab to the hotel, although she was only 8 blocks away. Noone she ran into spoke English. Emilia was tired from the trip, although she had gotten some sleep. Amir was glad to see her when he came by her room, the next day. They went out walking and talked constantly. The conference started the next day and lasted for three days. In the evenings, they usually walked after supper, as the sun does not set in Finland in the summertime; it remained light late at night. Emilia took pictures, and sketched buildings and waterfalls, and people while they talked. Amir was from Tehran, Iran. They had met in Praha in 1999, and continued to write for years. Reba had said that he wasn't happy with his wife, but Emilia doubted if he would ever divorce her because his religion didn't preclude having more than one wife. Still, the realization that the divorce was final next month and this gentleman was treating her like a lady, was exciting. When they parted, he wanted to know if she could go to Malaysia in the fall.

"I'd love to, Amir, but I will probably be having cataract surgery on my eyes." She had replied.

"Try, please, my dear," he implored.

"I will. Yes, I will try."

The congress was interesting and one neurologist that she knew from Scotland gave a very interesting talk on genetics and seizures. Another neurologist, who was originally from India, but lived in Wales, bought her new book, *The Swallow's Flight, Tales of Persons with Misunderstood Neurological Disorders*. Remembering the value of the euro in 2004, Emilia charged him 20 euros for the book. It seemed about right. She had intended to give a copy to Amir but he left before she had an opportunity. The last night they had hamburgers at a local place after talking with a woman who worked at the bistro for a while. Amir knew the town well. He pointed out several places that she was not familiar with and they walked all around the different statues that he pointed out. One was set up at the end of WWII.

"Do you think you can help me find a publisher for the book that I am writing?" he asked on the last night. "It is called *D Day*. I believe that unless people stop having so many children, the world will be too full of people. It will implode."

"That's an interesting thought," Emilia replied. "But yes, I can help you. Do you want it translated into English form Farsi?"

"Yes, yes. That is precisely what I want." Like Emilia, Amir's eyes lit up when he talked about his book. It had become very important to him, as his letters had indicated. He had already looked in England for a publisher, and he was going back there again later this summer.

When Emilia returned, she was able to locate someone who could translate Farsi into English. She gave her the name of several persons in New York to contact. Eventually, the calls were made, and Amir had a contact to help him.

* * *

Emilia found Leah at home when she arrived. Everyone was doing fine, apparently. Sheana and Moona were inseparable as always. Sheana stayed over at Moona's half of the time, because there wasn't that much room at Emilia's. In mid-July, Eugen's mother passed on in Minnesota from Parkinson's disease and he wanted to go back for the funeral. Sheana went with him, in case his schizophrenia kicked in. They had a safe trip, but didn't stay long. Emilia paid for their tickets, and wondered where the next money would come from. Reba's words haunted her. "If your children want something, a mother has to buy it for them." These words sounded like those Malia would have said. Reba had convinced her that they were soul sisters.

In September, Leah and her family moved to a new place. Nicole and Moona had had to find another place to live quickly. The two sisters moved into a large duplex on Howard Street in New Haven. It was close enough to walk to the hospital.

When Emilia kept her appointment with the opthalmologist in late August, he sent her directly to her partner. Surgery was scheduled for October for the first cataract and again in mid November for the second. She stayed quiet most of the fall. Painting was all that she could really do well. She stayed quiet, most of the fall; painting was all that she could really do well. After the first operation, Emilia was surprised at how much brighter all of the colours looked to her eyes. She looked at the pictures that she had painted the year before and noticed that they weren't as bright, although the work was good. Recently her paintings had had a dull cast to them. It was like a gift from God to regain her sight and be able to read again.

On the 28th of December, she got new glasses. She could see again. She had had to wear a patch on the second eye until then. Now, that she had survived cancer and cataract surgery, Emilia figured it was time to go back for her master's degree. She was still tired, but she went back anyway. The first class she took in January. She made an A in that class, and she felt hope. Next semester she would take epidemiology, biostatistics and policies for public health. Two classes she took for credit, and the third she audited at the school's request. Her eyes bothered her when she had to stay on the computer for over two hours, and try as she would, she couldn't work the SPSS program that went with the biostatistics. She could write the material about the statistics, but she couldn't operate the program correctly. At the close of the semester, she believed she had passed, but she had not. She couldn't take and pass the tests. This was nothing new. Tests had always held up her progress in graduate school.

During the last month they had had to go on Saturdays as well as once a week for class. The trips wore her out physically because she rode busses most of the time. Sometimes she got rides, but rarely on Saturdays. One fellow student took her home on occasion, but there was never any real assurance that he would. Her seizures had gotten worse over the semester, which was normal when she was tired and under pressure. These seizures were more confusions states. She would find herself walking places distractedly, not knowing who she was or what she was supposed to be doing. She had started having this type of seizure in 1997 when lemotragine and the generic clonazepam had been added to her regimen. The lemotragine had long since left her system, and the neurologist didn't seem to realize that the seizures she had were different, as they had not changed since she became his patient.

In the spring, she had sent in her paperwork to attend the Singapore ILAE Asian congress. She thought that Amir would be there. That spring, she had saved money for the congress because most of the bills Reba had run up, the previous year had been paid off. When she didn't have to worry about credit cards, her economy was fine. She was still paying a low amount on her mortgage, although she knew that if she didn't act this summer, the payment would escalate by $900 or more in October.

In June, she was contacted by a man from Nigeria who wanted to leave her a large sum of money. She got as much information as possible from him, and he got a great deal from her. However, when he asked for $7000.00 she paid it because she believed that he would pay her back. Reba had told her that she would be contacted by someone from another country who wanted to leave her money. Now that it had occurred, Reba couldn't be reached. When he asked for more money and she said, "No."

Feeling like a fool, she told Patrick, who laughed at her and told her to go to the police. Nicole drove her there, but the police wouldn't help her and gave her the phone number for the FBI. She left the police station and took the bus home. Emilia had had so many run-ins with the police when she and George were living in Minnesota that she had very little faith in the police doing anything positive for her. Her feeling was that someone should appreciate the material that she had accumulated about Haggaii, whom a friend had found was on the most wanted list from Nigeria.

Just as she got home, Reba turned up on her door-step with her husband. She insisted that they go to a casino in a near by town and get $500.00 from one MasterCard that she had not used at all. Emilia felt trapped. When they got back, Leah was waiting for her. Leah took one look at Reba and informed her mother that she was on crystal. Emilia respected her daughter's view because she knew Leah knew a druggie if she saw one. Reba and JW couldn't leave quickly enough.

This time, Emilia said nothing about going to Singapore. If Reba hadn't asked for money, she might have. Reba and JW had told her that they were living in Groton, CT and would be coming over a lot this summer.

Emilia asked her if she knew anything about Haggaii. She claimed that he was not the man she had been told would leave Emilia money. There must have been a mistake.

* * *

Section XI:

2007-2008

Chapter XXXVII

Emilia goes to Singapore

Emilia left the next week for Singapore. She flew through Detroit again, and then on to Tokyo where she waited for four hours and looked around the airport. She didn't have enough money to get more than one item in the airport. Prices in 2007 were higher than they had been in 2002, and much higher than they had been in 1985 when she had flown to India.

If they had flown over Hawaii, she had not been aware of it today. She enjoyed the Japanese food and tea, but she was growing tired. Soon she would be in Singapore. She had not heard from Amir and only knew that he would be there, nothing else. When she arrived, she found a beautiful tropical paradise that was reminiscent in color and foliage of Oahu or Kauaii. She soon realized that the humidity was prohibitively high. The best time to walk was early in the morning or late at night. Also, she found that to get to the conference hall, it was best to take the underground sidewalk that wound through the town and was air-conditioned.

Her hotel room faced the ocean which provided the opportunity to sketch and paint anytime. She brought her book with her and sold it to a woman from Spain on the third day of the conference when she was putting up her exhibit. She saw Amir only twice, and then not for long. He was staying on the other side of town, and never succeeded in making arrangements to meet her outside the conference.

While she was there, she broke down and got a new suit and a shirt, made of silk. Her new clothes felt good and looked good. The seamstress Sarah wanted to do a dress also. Later she would regret not doing it, but that day Emilia allowed her Scottish thrift to win and she held on to her money. The Episcopal Cathedral was next door to the hotel, and she went there on two occasions. They had fans, not air-conditioning, just like the church in New Haven.

Because of a typhoon that was hitting Japan; she flew back through The Netherlands, stopping in Amsterdam to change planes only a short time. This meant that she had to wait an extra twenty-four hours to catch the flight, but the airport put her up in a nearby hotel. She didn't like it that much, and had to spend money on food for she realized that the plane might not serve food. However, they did. This flight was flying over Europe, so they served food. She got back the same day that she had left, as she gained a day flying over Europe.

When she found in August that she would not be accepted at SCSU graduate program, she decided to try a Masters Degree in Psychology online. Earlier, she had set up the FAFSA grant needed for economic assistance through the University of Phoenix Online. It would take 21 months they said to conclude the program which would enable her to teach in a four-year college or online. Also, she would have the MA degree after her name when she published her next book.

Emilia realized that she wanted to travel as a professor or a research person, rather than a person who had epilepsy. She had felt that a part of her life was drawing to a close, so she told herself not to be disappointed if she didn't get to Africa in 2008. By the end of August, she had concluded a new mortgage that paid off the $7000 bill she had run up with the Nigerian, and $4000.00 she and Reba had run up on her Target card, as well as settling a 40-year mortgage that was fixed, something that she had been trying to accomplish since 2000 when she first began getting money through refinancing. The mortgage included taxes, which was what she had wanted, but it was $1997.04, which was about $500 more than her payments had been. Still, at last, she had very little credit card debt and that was a relief. She believed that she was going to turn her life around. Emilia had concluded that Reba was more of a liability than an asset, but she still thought of her as a friend. She realized that her family believed that she was wrong to trust Reba, and there were times when Emilia did not trust her and wanted to end their relationship. Yet, she wanted to know where her brother was as well.

She began the classes towards her Masters degree in Psychology through the University of Phoenix online that September. Things were moving quickly. She was full of hope for the future. Next month, she would begin paying on the new mortgage. Her future began to look good.

Chapter XXXVIII

Emilia goes to Boston to end it with Reba

Reba called Emilia in mid October, telling her that she wouldn't be able to meet with her, but it was essential that Emilia come to Boston and have lunch with Shannon who would take her where she needed to go. Everything with Reba was shrouded with mystery. Emilia enjoyed the mystery to a point. She did not enjoy being ridiculed by people who were convinced that she was being conned, when she believed that she was doing the right thing. She informed Reba, that she had no money; and if Reba wanted her to come, she would have to arrange to pay $100 to her to cover the AMTRAK bill. Reba agreed.

When she arrived at Back Bay Station, JW and Shannon picked her up forty-five minutes late. He dropped them across from Lord and Taylor's Salon. First he begrudgingly handed over the $100 that Reba had promised.

* * *

"It's pleasant having lunch with you, Emilia, without Reba." Shannon said as she steered Emilia across the busy street. Emilia was always amazed at how often pedestrians in Boston jay-walked.

"She makes me nervous these days. I can never tell whether or not she can be trusted."

"Oh, I noticed that she had changed last August," Emilia said.

"I don't even like to leave the children with them."

"That's unfortunate. I still haven't seen the baby."

"She's three now."

"They grow up fast, don't they?" Emilia said. "Does this place have good sandwiches?"

"Order what ever you want."

"Thanks, maybe I will," Emilia replied. She picked something that would fill her up because she had no idea when she would get home. After lunch, they went to Lord and Taylor's and picked out the things that Reba had reserved. Then they walked to Boston Common and sat and talked for a while. Half an hour later, Stacey turned up with a message for both of them. They were to go into the building across the street and Emilia was supposed to charge her card for whatever the man had set aside for her.

"What is this place?" Emilia asked.

"It's the place Reba told me to take you to," Shannon answered. Stacey, Reba's older daughter-in-law had left, claiming that she had errands to run.

In the shop, Emilia realized that the man was selling her gold bars. She signed the paper work, and left it with him. He would give everything to Shannon the next day, he said.

"Are you sure you want to do this, Miss?"

"I don't have any choice," Emilia replied.

After they had completed the negotiation, Emilia realized that she never wanted to work with these people again. Something was beginning to feel extremely wrong.

* * *

On November 23rd, just before Thanksgiving Day, Reba called again. This time, she wanted to see Emilia in Boston immediately. She could be very persuasive when she needed to be, and Emilia felt compelled not to question her. She had never enjoyed paying for Reba's Spirits' spending jags. But once they were alone, Reba owned her will. That day, she had a bad feeling when she walked into what had been *"La Fonda's"*, the Mexican restaurant and smelled a horrible odor. It seemed like an ill omen.

It was cold, and the new owner was redoing the floors with all of the windows closed, as it was snowing outside. Eventually, Reba arrived and they went across the street to another place. Emilia kept telling Reba that she could not spend money today. Reba, never paid her any mind, but continued to tell JW where to take them.

"Now, Emilia, we are going to shop till we drop today. YOU HAVE TO DO THIS. IT IS THE LAST THING YOU HAVE TO DO FOR THE WORK. Listen to me. I have your best interests at heart. We are sisters through the spirit. You want to meet your brother, don't you? You want to know who the rich man is, don't you?"

"Yes, but I don't have any money to spend. Don't you understand that?"

"You always find a way to land on your feet. Remember how I fooled the trust? Oh, was your mother happy that day!"

"Reba, how do I know that you actually talk to spirits?"

"Haven't I arranged for you to see some things, yourself?"

"Yes." Emilia remembered the dream that she had had about one man who still remained nameless. The sex was to die for. Suddenly, she realized that it wasn't the first such dream she had had. Dreams like those had transpired when she was in Minnesota before she ever laid eye on Reba. She realized that she had related material to this woman that she wouldn't have told her own children at that time. Suddenly, Emilia was no longer able to fight with Reba. She wanted to end the work, and get back what belonged to her. More importantly, Emilia wanted to leave town.

After shopping in Boston, Reba had JW drive Emilia to Medford where they purchased furniture that Reba had already ordered. Next they went to Circuit City, a company that Emilia refused to patronize. She had had bad experiences with them.

"What do you want to buy in this place?" Emilia asked with disdain.

"Don't get so uppity. If you are angry, the work cannot be finished. Cheer up, Emilia, we are almost through. This is the last purchase you will make."

"Do you realize that you will have purchased material through 13 of my credit cards tonight, if we buy anything here? What do you want from me anyway?"

"A TV-Video to use in Canada at the nunnery where I am staying, and you can even see the video that I will take with it," Reba chirped.

"JW, what happened to the last TV she bought when you lived at 35 Kingston St. in Boston?" Emilia asked.

"Oh, that TV exploded." Reba said brightly. "Didn't I tell you?"

"No. You never mentioned it. When you lived on Kingston St, it seemed to work alright to me," Emilia continued.

"WE HAVE TO GET THIS." Reba shouted.

Emilia's patience was blown. She felt as though she had been held hostage since she got into their car. She determined to conclude the evening's purchases and return to Back Bay Station as soon as possible. There she would board the next train back to Connecticut before morning. It was growing later and later. She was hungry, and asked if they could stop and eat, but Reba didn't have any money. Reba continued to insist that Emilia buy a TV that she could use in the woods to video-tape a scene of Emilia that appeared in one of the trees there.

Emilia had heard wild stories, but this was beyond belief. She said as much. She refused to pay, and she did not have a credit-card for Circuit City. Finally, in desperation Reba agreed to pay her back everything in two weeks. That said, Emilia bought the TV, and JW drove her back to the train station.

She believed for two weeks that Reba would pay her back, but in mid December, as the bills began to arrive, she began to call debt collection people who could help her pay back the money that she had charged on 13 credit cards that fateful day. She determined that this time, she would pay it off without looking to another for help. She knew full well that the reason that her mortgage was so high was partially because of Reba's spending. She couldn't understand how she had been deceived again and again by this woman.

When she called to inquire why she hadn't heard from Reba, Shannon's husband told her that his mother had returned to Canada and they did not know when she would return. His father was gone also. He offered Emilia little help.

From December of 2007 through April of 2008, Emilia played Russian roulette with the credit card people and the debt counselors. She went through 7 companies in that period of time, in an endeavor to keep everyone happy. She estimated that she paid out easily $1000 a month in an attempt to find a company that wouldn't con her as the Credit Counselors of America had done three years earlier.

In January, Reba called and asked for $1000.00. Emilia told she didn't have it and hung up. That was the last time that she talked to Reba until June. Another man sounding like Haggaii called her from England, telling her that she had been left money by a particular person and he would arrange to have her sent the money for a price. She strung him on long enough to get all of his information. Then she forwarded it to the

FBI, who showed little interest. When he wanted her to meet him at the airport, she said "No," and stopped answering the home phone, doing most of her business on her cell phone.

Emilia was still going to school. She had gone through two courses in statistics successfully in the spring, and she was elated by the fact that her grades were higher than they had ever been.

In April, George came over to Nicole's new home for Easter dinner. They had a pleasant time talking. He even walked around with his cane a little. Everyone had a great time. Leah, Eugen, and the children, and Nicole, Moona, Emilia and George enjoyed one another's company. Even Boo-boo the cat seemed to like George.

* * *

The next week Emilia called Leah and Eugen and asked them to come over and talk with her. She needed to tell someone what she was planning, and Emilia had no reason to believe that Nicole would understand how badly she felt. She and Leah had always been on the same wave length.

They sat down at the table in the dining room, and Emilia poured everyone coffee.

"I have to tell you all something that is embarrassing and upsetting. I should have told you earlier, but I figured you all had enough on your plate."

"Are you ill, Mom?" Eugen asked.

"No, aside from the confusion seizures that won't leave me. No, my health is fine. As you know, from meeting Reba, I should never have trusted her as I have. I figure, over the years, she has absconded about $212,000.00 from me one way or another."

Leah opened her mouth, but no sound came out.

"She's a psychic and when I met her the first time, I had just come back from Europe in 1996. You all were here when the doctors at Yale put me on half the strength of Klonopin, and changed it to the generic version. I have always felt that that was a bad move."

"I remember. You weren't yourself for quite a while." Leah said. "Remember how Simon made your hospital bed go up and down."

"Yes. He was a card." Emilia smiled. "One of the reasons my mortgage is so high now is because I used the money from the mortgages to pay off the bills that she and the nursing home had run up. I am afraid that we will lose quite a bit of money, but there may be a way around it that I haven't figured out yet.

"How did she get so much money out of you?" Eugen asked.

"She claimed that it was for the work, which was supposed to help me get over seizures, and make a lot of money. It sounds like what those con artists in Nigeria tried too. I can't believe that I fell for them too. What I don't understand is why I fell for it."

"Don't be so hard on yourself, Mother." Leah said. "Dad is taking a lot out of you emotionally."

"Apparently, he is taking a lot out of Reba, too," Emilia laughed. "Reba was sure that getting him here to Connecticut would make it easier for her to control him. I told her not to fool with his spirit, and she didn't listen."

"Serves her right," Leah said. "I would like to go up there and beat her up."

"You'd land in jail. Besides, she's still in Canada. I haven't heard anything from her since January of this year, when she called to ask for more money."

"You didn't send her any did you?"

"Hell, no," Emilia replied. "I appreciate your not putting me down. I have tried to be more careful of her since she talked to you last summer, and you said she looked as though she were on crystal. You know she used to ask me for clonazepam. Claimed it was for the work, that she wasn't taking it. I guess I am gullible."

"Don't worry, Mother," Leah sighed, "so am I. It runs in the family."

"This spring has been hard for me, because I have tried to find a company that wouldn't take all of my money while they helped me pay off the creditors. I have gone through six companies so far. Tomorrow, I am calling a seventh company. You don't know this but several years ago, I had a similar problem, and tried to pay it all off. One company took quite a bit of money from me, but didn't pay the creditors. I had to ask for assistance that time. This time, I am not asking for help from anyone unless they owe me money, like Reba's family.

"Maybe we could go up there and persuade her to give us the things you bought and sell them on E-bay." Leah said. "It's worth a shot."

"We don't know where they are. She is still in Canada. Her family is not going to help us, although I like her daughter in law."

"Mother, she was part of the scheme. Did you ever call the police?"

"Here? No. Most of the things she did occurred in Massachusetts; only a couple of things occurred in Connecticut. Besides, they would laugh at me. I did consider calling the Medford police, but I didn't go through with it"

"Maybe you should," Eugen put in. "Mom, people take advantage of kind hearted persons like you. Everyone wants money. Some people don't care how they get it."

"I reckon that's right, Eugen," Emilia said. "Would you like any more coffee?"

"No. We've got to go though. We love you, Mom. You just have to take care of yourself." Getting up, Eugen came over and hugged Emilia. He was a tall man and he cared about Emilia.

"Yeah, the boys have been alone long enough." Leah said. Sheana is over at Nicole's today studying with Moona.

* * *

Later that week, Emilia came across a gentleman from Amsterdam who worked for the seventh debt counseling company. By then, some of the companies were threatening to take her to court.

"You have to file bankruptcy, Mrs. Blake. It's the only way. I wouldn't let my mother go through what that woman has put you through. I can't imagine a person charging off 13 credit cards in one night to the tune of $39,000. It's ridiculous. Now, promise me, you will seek bankruptcy."

"There is no other way?"

"Do you want to continue paying her bills?"

"No. She's gotten enough from me. I do not want to do that." Emilia said.

After she hung up the phone, she called the man that Patrick had referred her to. He charged $750 for the initial visit. After tearing up the card in disgust, Emilia opened the yellow pages. She found someone quickly who lived close by and was on a bus route. She called the office and set up an appointment with him for the following day. He didn't charge that much initially. She had time to collect the money she needed to pay him.

In an effort to get money from Reba's son, she sent the Medford police over to their home. After a raucous conversation, Shannon agreed to pay $1500.00, which was about the amount that she needed to pay the attorney. That was a start, at least.

Her attorney told her she was not to pay any more at all. He wanted a list of all of her assets and all of her debts. Things seemed to be moving right along. Emilia was surprised at how relieved she began to feel.

Chapter XXXIX

George dies

Late in April, George was hospitalized at Milford Hospital with pneumonia. The girls were over there constantly, but he seemed well enough to be sent back home after a week. After three days, he returned with a worse case of pneumonia. This time, Emilia visited him at the nurses' request. What she saw was horrifying. George was constantly shaking. The entire bed shook continuously. He only moaned; but you could see the pain in his eyes. He could no longer talk, swallow, or breathe on his own. The pneumonia had escalated the Parkinson's disease dramatically. The nurses had contacted her because they felt that he should be given hospice treatment immediately. After this type of reaction to the combined problems of pneumonia and Parkinson's disease, his body had worn itself out.

When George had entered the hospice area, Emilia called Francis, Rose, and Neil. Neil had decided that they would drive out. They arrived a few hours after his passing. He brought Francis, their brother Alfe's wife with him. His sister Rose wasn't strong enough to make the trip. Emilia had been writing her repeatedly to let her know how everything was going. She had also kept in touch with George's son Rudy, who was a year younger than Neil. Rudy didn't want to come, if his father died, nor did Yenta.

Later that night, they started him on a low dose of morphine that would ease his pain. Emilia supposed that it was similar to her father's situation when he died. Three days later, George was moved to the hospice area of the hospital. The family was allowed to stay at night if they liked, as there were plenty of chairs to rest in. Eugen and Leah and Nicole took turns sitting with him constantly. Emilia finally came over again on May 2nd and stayed 24 hours, leaving at 6:00 a. m. the following morning.

She didn't go into his room at first except to peep in and see how the children were doing. He seemed quiet at last. George began to look calm, something that had not occurred for years. Leah commented that he reminded her of her Grandfather, Alfred Blake, when he was dying. He did resemble him, Emilia thought.

That day, she had painted all day and late into the night. At 10 p.m., she had gone into his room and stayed with George rocking him and singing to him the song her grandmother loved to sing to her when she was ill, *"Tura. Lura, Lura, Tura Lura Lai."* It was Emilia's Grandmother's favorite melody, and she had played the record by John McCormick, the Irish Tenor she loved for years. Emilia had sung this same song to Simon when he was in ICU for five weeks after being born with only one functioning lung. Eventually, Simon's lungs had grown and functioned, but for five weeks it had been touch and go.

Emilia was surprised by the fact that she wanted to stay with George, singing and playing with his hair for as long as she did. In his room, all people had to wear gloves, masks and protective gear. She didn't bother with the mask, but wore the other things. Apparently, he had developed another infection as well. The children were asleep in the other room of the Hospice area and didn't disturb them.

Emilia came out and talked with the nurses twice, and returned until she finally left his room exhausted about 3 a.m. Even so, she could not sleep. When Nicole got there at 6 a.m., she took her home. Emilia didn't go back. Later that morning, George passed on as Eugen sat with him. Leah and Nicole had gone out for a smoke. Eugen said he looked calm when he went. Francis and Neil arrived from South Dakota before George was taken from the room.

*   *   *

Emilia had already talked with several funeral homes. They didn't plan to have the service in a funeral home, as George wished to be buried at sea. Cremation was suggested. He had always wanted to be dropped into the ocean, and the U.S. Navy was willing to do this, but they couldn't do it in Connecticut because he had served his country on destroyers, not submarines. Sailors who had served their country on destroyers were put to rest in San Diego, or Virginia Beach, complete with a video for the family.

Leah thought that they could put him into the water themselves. She wanted to be sure that he made it to the ocean. She had called Yenta when he died. Emilia was sorry that Yenta had not come, but she understood why she didn't. Having Neil and Frances there made it easier. They had a small service in the chapel of the church they had attended. Bary, the minister who had suggested that they live together officiated. Jana was the only one besides the family that was there.

Frances suggested that they design a little pamphlet about George's life and had copies printed before the service. They used a picture taken at the last Navy reunion he attended in 2004, which Emilia had.

Neil arranged for a tribute to George from the Navy to be sent back to South Dakota so that they could place it at the family grave site, near their family's grave. He felt that the thirty years his brother had spent in the Navy should be recognized. He also talked with Rudy on his return.

After the service, they went to the park near Emilia and George's home and took pictures. Later, they went to West Haven and had dinner at Turk's, a local seafood restaurant that served excellent food. Dinner was Emilia's treat. Everyone seemed to relax and mellow out as they ate and visited. Neil and Francis had never met Leah and Eugen's two boys before, and they enjoyed them tremendously. Their seafood was good.

Afterwards, they went out to the veteran's area of the West Haven water-front and walked out by the water. It was chilly that night and a light sweater felt good to Emilia, as she walked across the beach and looked at the Memorial to the Vietnam Veterans. Neil took the boys out on the rocks.

* * *

Two weeks later, Kelly, one of Leah's friends died in Minnesota. She flew back alone. It was a double blow for her. It would take Leah a long time to recover from the deaths. Leah had insisted on keeping the ashes until they were put into the ocean.

Because of George's death, the attorney handling her bankruptcy held up the procedure until he was certain that Emilia would receive nothing from George's estate . . . The state took everything that it could. The children got $34.92 each later that year. Emilia did get an increase in social security which was helpful.

It would be November 2nd before Emilia, Leah and Eugen scattered George's ashes in the Harbor in New Haven, out where Leah and Nicole liked to go sunbathing with their families. Leah took the ashes out into the water. The waves rose up to get them as if they had been waiting for them. Leah almost fell on the slippery strand she was balancing on. Afterwards, everyone felt better. Emilia felt a sense of fulfillment, and Leah felt as though a great precipice had receded

Chapter XL

Bankruptcy, school, and generic medication
Fall of 2008

In July, Emilia began taking the generic Mebaral. She reasoned it would be cheaper. She continued to feel tired. In August her family doctor gave her injections of B12 and told her she must take it daily until her next appointment in November. Emilia took the B12 as requested this time; but it didn't seem to help. She remained tired. Her seizures increased as well. For a while in June, they had been fine, but humidity usually created problems, so she didn't think much about the fact that she was now taking two generic medications.

In October, Emilia began working for a lawyer doing medical illustration. She did a lot of research on the topic at Yale's medical library. One day, when she was walking over to the medical library, she stopped and sat down as she felt the seizure beginning. It didn't last long, and she tried to take the medication, but dropped it. When the seizures left, she took the medication and ate some food she had purchased just before she blanked out. She had two more seizures that day, as she walked to the library. When she got to the library, she felt anxious. She drew and painted for three hours and then caught the bus home.

The following day, she had to get ink for her computer in a different area of town. After purchasing the ink, Emilia decided to stop for coffee and lunch and read part of her assignment. The weather was pleasant, and she decided to walk over to the attorney's office. After cris-crossing the blocks she came to Trumbull Street. As she was about to cross over a dirt walk, a bad seizure struck. She sat down and waited for it to pass.

She had no idea where she was, who she was or what she should be doing. It was hard to tell how long it lasted because she began to move before it had cleared. She walked down five more blocks and went into a grocery store to get out of the heat. While she was there, she realized she was having another seizure. When she came out of it, she had forgotten what she had intended to buy, so she left. Four blocks later, a bad seizure that made her feel that she had no knowledge of whom she was, only that she had to keep walking, struck again. She kept going until she had crossed the street. Realizing that she was going the wrong way, she stopped. As she was coming out of it, she sat down and rested until she was certain where she was, what she was going to do, and if she still had the material that she had originally. When she felt better, she got up and crossed the street, which was busy, as it was mid-afternoon. Then she crossed the next main street and went on to the attorney's office. When Emilia arrived, she still couldn't talk well. She sank into the chair by the door, and drank some water the secretary gave her. When her attorney was ready to see her, she gave him the information he had requested. As it was late in the day, and she had explained what had happened while she was walking over, he suggested that he take her home. She was grateful for the offer.

The same problem of three seizures in one day happened again a week or so later. It always occurred over a week-end, or when her doctor wasn't available, she noticed. To her dismay, he never returned her calls. Finally, Emilia quit calling him. This wasn't the first time that her neurologist hadn't returned her calls, nor would it be the last. He worked at Yale now. He had been in Farmington, at UCONN Med Center when she first began seeing him. Then she would see him whenever there was a problem like this, and someone from the centre would call to check on her if it continued. Yale had a different policy though, and she had to deal with the nurse before she could get through to the doctor.

In early November, her pharmacist had suggested that maybe the generic Mebaral was not working for her. She told him that she would wait another month and see if the problems continued.

For a while, the seizures decreased. Then she got her flu shot, and she got sick again. Leah gave her some Sudafed for her throat when she was over for supper around the tenth of November. The weather was turning cold again and then it would warm up. Good weather for pneumonia. Emilia took about 22 of the Sudafed over 15 days. She seemed to be feeling better, and her spirits seemed high. However, her throat still ached. Finally, three days before Thanksgiving, she received a call from someone informing her that she had won the Reader's Digest Sweepstakes for Connecticut. She had received this call before in the summer and discounted it because it was supposed to be offered in the late fall, or early December. Twice before that month, she had received calls about other such prizes. In September Emilia had been told that her identity had been stolen by an employee of the company that held her mortgage, and warned to contact the police if anything unusual occurred. Twice the phone calls had come from Jamaica. The call that Monday came from Dallas. That night, Emilia felt as though Dave, this person from Dallas could be trusted. He was from Texas, after all, and he acted and sounded like a gentleman. He even told her that some of the companies that offered her ways to make money were con artists. He portrayed himself as a person who could be trusted, and when he told her the amount of the winning, she was stunned. At that point, she could use money to pay off the mortgage. She still had not concluded the bankruptcy. More important than that was the desire to help her children and grandchildren have a better life. Sheana had begun college that fall, and her mother was working double shifts to pay for the tuition. Sheana wanted to be a doctor's assistant, and Emilia felt that she would succeed in her desire. By then, Moona had gotten herself in the family way with her boyfriend Isaiah Jackson. Emilia was not surprised. Moona was a lot like she had been. They had both been raised as only children, and she remembered wanting desperately to have her own home where someone would love and take care of her. She believed that Moona felt the same way. The fact that things had not worked out that well, was beside the point. She understood why her granddaughter got pregnant. Emilia's mother had stressed the importance of virginity to the point that Emilia had wanted to rebel, but had not. The abuse George showed them had prevented his daughters from understanding that he cared.

 The next day Dave and another man called stating that he was with Lords of London and would be making certain that the money that was rightfully hers would be awarded to her. He went on to tell her that she must send money by Western Union or Money Gram to the address in Costa Rica that he would give her.

 "Look, I can't get in my car and run down to Wal-Mart and send this as you suggested," Emilia replied.

 "Why not?"

 "I don't drive and I don't have a car."

"Can you send it by Western Union?"

"Only if I do it over the phone," Emilia replied. "While she was talking with the man, she dialed the number on a card from a banker at Chase. When the person answered, she held her cell phone down to the house phone so that he could hear what was said:

"This is Emilia Blake. I need help. Listen to this conversation."

"What was that noise?" Kevin asked.

"What did it sound like?"

"Frankly, miss, I couldn't understand a word that was said."

Emilia hung up, because Alex, the man from Las Vegas was screaming that she should tell no one what their conversation was about. He informed her that he would call back in an hour and he hoped that she would have sent the information to the people in Costa Rica by then.

"You still haven't given me their name or their address," she said as the phones went dead.

Next, she called the bank back, and asked for Maria.

"There's no Maria here." Kevin replied.

"She should be there, she handles the fraud department."

"Oh, you want the Wall Street branch. You have the wrong branch."

"What is their number?"

"Here: 203-444-8868. What's going on?"

"Frankly, I don't know," Emilia replied. Suddenly, she didn't want to deal with the situation any longer.

She called the number that he had given her.

"Hello, this is Michelle. I'm really busy. What do you want?"

"Michelle, I need to talk to Maria."

"She's busy. We're all busy. The place is packed. Call back in an hour."

Emilia looked at the cell phone and said. "Look, I need help. You are supposed to help me, but you really don't care about your customers anyway, do you?"

She got up and went over to the dresser and got out her Western Union card. She figured Alex would call her back before long, and if she had to do this alone, she'd do the best that she could.

Instead, Dave called her. She told him what had happened. She also told him that she didn't trust Alex.

"Wait, wait. Let me handle Alex. I want to get you all set up so that you have all the money you and your family need. I'll take care of Alex. Trust me; I'll call you back in a half hour."

"OK."

"Smile. Things will work out." Dave said and rang off.

Sure enough in 30 minutes Alex was back on the line, giving her the correct information for Costa Rica, and assuring her of the exact amount, the reason for the need to send the money to Costa Rica, as well as answers to questions she had not formulated yet.

Emilia sent close to $4000.00 in two payments that day. She believed that she had enough in her account to cover that amount and still cover the mortgage.

Dave called her back at 10 p.m. to tell her that she would be receiving the package with the money tomorrow, as it was being flown to Connecticut.

Emilia was too afraid that something would go wrong to tell her daughter Leah of the situation when she called. Instead, she acted as though nothing was going on at all.

Then she called Kathe, her friend in Plano, Texas. "I am going to get money, Kathe. I know it. I won the sweepstakes for Connecticut's Reader's Digest award."

"Congratulations, Emilia." Kathe said. "Call me back tomorrow?"

"Sure."

To her surprise, that night she slept well. She was happy and she felt as though she were on cloud nine. "We're going to be rich, Pepper," she said while she was eating supper. "I can give the money to the Epilepsy Foundation that I want to, and still pay off the mortgage and pay for Sheana's college."

Pepper who had looked at the phone constantly with distrust was not enthusiastic. However, he nuzzled Emilia, to show his concern. He didn't trust the voices that upset his owner. The phone that people were calling on was a speaker phone. If anyone had come over there, they would have been detected. Emilia wasn't sure why, but she trusted Dave.

The next day, Dave called early to tell her that he was upset with the situation. Brinks Security was planning to charge her $3000 because they hadn't been able to find her apartment the day before. Instead, they had stayed in a hotel, and had run up a high bill.

Emilia still believed him, but she realized that if she did this, she could go broke. Then, for no reason that she could fathom, she decided not to be afraid and gamble with her funds.

Later in the day, a third man called her from Memphis, TN. He told her in no uncertain terms that she had not won second prize, but first, and the money had to be returned and recounted before she could receive it. He went on to tell her that it was important for her to send $3000 at once to an address that she would receive on the next phone call.

When Alex called back, Emilia took down the information and then recalled Chase. This time, she got Machelle again and asked her what her balance was. She was assured that she had over $3000 in her account. She asked again for Maria, but was told that she had gone home.

Emilia sent the money to the people in Costa Rica. By ten that night, she realized that she had been conned. Dave never called back. "Alex," who had called 16 times earlier that day, "was in a meeting," she was told by a new voice, a young African American. He assured her that everything would be taken care of and she would be called again.

At 10:30 she reported the entire incident to the Western Union Fraud department. They told her that they would try to get the money back, but weren't sure if they could. Earlier when she had called with the names of one person, she had been told that he had not picked up his mail. She hoped that he still had not done so.

* * *

The next morning was Thanksgiving Day. Emilia called the police and a pleasant man came over and took the report. She explained that she had received phone calls from people like these people for four months solid, and finally she had cracked. She wanted to help her family.

The officer told her that wanting to help one's family was fine, but today people took advantage of older women whom they believed had money.

Emilia was thankful that he had not made fun of her as the police officer who had come in 2007 had. She dressed carefully, as Nicole had said that they would pick her up early in the morning for Dinner. She called back at 12:00 noon to tell her that it was going to be late, because Leah and Eugen didn't get the turkey on early.

Emilia asked her daughter to pick her up about 4:00 so she could spend some time with Moona. She had a good time that night, in spite of the situation with the money. She had called four different people, trying to find someone who could help her make money by selling things, and reached only one. He had told her to call back later. When she did, he couldn't help her, as his son was very ill.

Emilia told him that she would pray for his son. When she hung up, she sent an e-mail to *The Circle of Caring* at her church and asked for prayers for her friend's son. It was the least that she could do.

* * *

Kathe had told her that on Tuesday she had sounded manic when she called her. She had confessed everything to her before she told her daughter what had happened. Somehow, she managed to pay the mortgage, as well as the electric and gas bill before the money that she had sent to Costa Rica was deducted from her account at the bank. Eventually, the money she got from social security, her pension, and $600 sent from the trust, paid off the major part of her debt to the bank. However, the remaining bills were returned unpaid.

The next day, she called Leah and Eugen and asked them to come over. She was in tears when she called. She suddenly realized that she was stone broke. Somehow, the mortgage payment and the electrical bill had been paid. That she found out from the website at Chase. All of the other checks would be returned.

They came over after Leah got off work, about 6 or so. Leah took her in her arms and let her sob out the story, ending by saying that she had done it for the children. As Emilia said this, she thought how Daniel had always done things 'for the children'. He seemed to have claimed her daughters and grandchildren as his own, although he had never allowed her to get too close to him. Still he had cared.

Suddenly the phone rang. It was Alex, the telephone caller from Las Vegas. Leah, who by then knew the situation, told him to get lost in no uncertain terms. Then Eugen stepped up to the phone and continued on for 15 minutes non-stop. All Alex could say was: "I am from Lords of London; you cannot talk to me that way."

"I just did." Eugen continued. "Don't you ever mother-fuckin' call my mother-in-law again!"

Interestingly enough, he hung up, and never placed another call to Emilia Blake.

"I guess I told him off," Eugen said.

"I'm just glad you were here," Emilia replied.

They went back into the dining room and had something to eat and Eugen told Emilia that she had to change her phone numbers that day. While they were talking, she changed the cell phone, but she had to wait until Monday to change the house phone, because the AT&T office was closed over the week-end. Suddenly, Emilia didn't feel so all alone.

"I knew something was wrong with you yesterday, Mother," Leah said.

"How?" Emilia asked.

"I can tell when you aren't yourself and you were too quiet yesterday. I knew something was eating at you. I figured you'd talk to me when you decided to. And you did."

"Yes, I did. Thank you for understanding."

"Do you understand that I love you, whatever happens, I will always love you for being you."

"Really?"

"Yes, really . . ."

"I guess so many people have said that and recanted their word that I don't believe people care anymore." Emilia said. "I guess it's silly."

"No, you've been hurt a lot over the years and so have I. That's one reason I understand."

"I talked to Theo and Yenta yesterday. Theo called me twice."

"How are they?"

"They seem to be doing OK. Theo told me that I should contact the Attorney General, and I told him that Eugen had made the same comment. He seemed in rare form." Emilia said.

* * *

After everyone had left, Emilia called the family doctor. She told him that she had been on two generic anticonvulsants and taken Sudafed for a throat infection. She believed that the combination had created bad side effects. He agreed that it was possible, and advised her not to take Sudafed any more. He also put the drug down in her chart so that it would not be ordered by accident.

After she hung up, Emilia decided that she would order Mebaral and begin the regular drug in December. By now, there were only a few days left in November, and it was time to reorder medicine anyway. Then she called her neurologist, but was given his nurse's voice mail. Next she called her insurance broker to see if there were ways to obtain the brand name drugs at a lower price.

He agreed to look into it, and advised her to get onto the medication as quickly as possible. When she talked with Jay, whom she had known since the 1980s, she suggested that Emilia find a new doctor. That sounded refreshing.

Looking in the yellow pages, she found Southern Connecticut Neurological Association, and called them. After explaining that she needed a neurologist who was familiar with complex partial seizures that secondarily generalized, and a physician who had a partner who could take over if he were out of town, she was given an appointment in 6 weeks on January 6th.

At this point, Emilia believed that there was a possibility that generic drugs had been the key to many of her problems. The problems with confusion seizures, walking seizures, as well as the inability to see a con artist at work had begun in 1997 when she had been placed on clonazepam, the generic Klonopin. Prior to that, she had been able to out-con the cons. She remembered the haunting words of Charles Gibbs who had recently died. He was a pharmacist and friend from East Texas who had continually said: "Don't take the generic Klonopin, it is not safe. I don't trust it."

* * *

Emilia began working on Mary Kay orders in dead earnest. In December the only income that she had was from Mary Kay sales. She made approximately $200 that month on sales.

When Emilia realized how badly she had allowed herself to be conned, she vowed to find out why it had occurred. In mid December, the neurologist returned her call of late November. By that time, she had found another doctor who could give her a second opinion. She returned to the brand name Mebaral, and in January she returned to the brand name Klonopin. The banker who handled her trust decided to take over her bills for a while until they found what was causing her to give money away. After Emilia was on both brand name drugs, her seizures changed back to the type that she had had before her medication had been changed in 1997. She was no longer depressed, even though she was broke at Christmas, she was happy.

Chapter XLI

Financial Winter Worries

When she talked with Chase bank the Monday after Thanksgiving, the bank insisted that she did not need to change her accounts, as there were adequate funds in all of them.

The next day, she received a notice that her check had bounced. She returned to the bank and talked with another banker. Maria was still gone. That person did help her set up new accounts, as well as an online checking account, but by then, her social security, her pension, and a $600 check from a different bank had all been confiscated by the Chase bank to pay for her debt to the bank.

Emilia was furious with the bank and changed banks. She moved across the street, and wrote out a check for $25 to open the account. The banker told her that she would not cash it. Emilia had placed $20 in the Chase bank to open a new account there. One of her customers had paid her $80 on the first of December. She had about $5.00 in change for bus fare, but that was it. Now, she had to get enough medicine to last through December. Emilia's medication ran $138.00 for the brand name Mebaral. She paid the pharmacist $33.00 to cover 5 days, and called the banker who handled her other funds to see how she should pay for this. She told her that her money had been taken, and all that she had was about 50 dollars for the rest of the month.

That Christmas, Emilia still only had what was left of the $80.00 she had made from Mary Kay in her pocket. But for the first time in many years she was happy. Amir was always telling her to be happy, and until now, she had forgotten for eleven years how good it felt to be able to roll with the tide and take whatever came along.

Although for years, she gave the appearance of being happy, she hadn't been.

It was as though when she went onto the clonazepam, the generic Klonopin, she lost the ability to understand what her therapist had taught her: That she must always look to the future, and not look behind. That had been the way that George and Reba simultaneously had snagged her back into their arms. Reba had wanted George near, so that she could work on him. However, she found and was still finding out that his spirit was nothing with which to trifle.

On Christmas Eve, Emilia walked to church in the snow. It was cold, but she was dressed for the weather and enjoyed the walk. That night her final walking seizure occurred and for two blocks she wasn't sure who she was, although she corrected the direction in which she was walking. She encountered an old friend on the way who stopped to talk. Once she reached the church, she went in and ate the food that she had brought with her and read.

One of the alter guild women brought her home that night after the last service that she helped usher. Seizures became less frequent. This had been the first that week. Emilia had been busy in December with her studies which continued until December 22, 2008, the Alter Guild work, and the children. Everyone went to Leah and Eugen's the Saturday after Christmas because both girls were working on Christmas Day. So they celebrated later. She had done shopping before she ran through the money, and found some other things in the house.

Moona gave her a tea pot, Leah gave her a cup, and Nicole gave her a candle. That went together nicely. She was surprised at how peaceful she felt. She realized how precious friends and family were. That was what Christmas was all about anyway.

*   *   *

It took a lot of interacting and a lot of faith on the part of Emilia and the new trust officer but they managed to arrive at a situation that would be workable. The fact that the mortgage check, which had been $2,023.08 had gone through was a miracle to both of them. Everything else that Emilia owed was much less. Her utilities were under $600, the phone bill was being waived for a month because she had gotten new numbers, and only the condo bill was high. Other things, like expenses Emilia had to pay annually, could be postponed until January.

Leah had been afraid that she would have to act as an executrix of her mother's funds until Emilia and the banker worked out this plan. Gina, who was new to the Bank of Texas, already knew that Emilia had epilepsy and that she believed that the drugs mixed with the Sudafed had made her manic or unable to reason.

The trust officer agreed to help Emilia sort things out until she got her medication under control and they were sure that she was no longer vulnerable to con artists. Someone else might never have believed that the generic drugs were the key to her problems, although she had had problems for 11 years.

Emilia wrote, painted and sold Mary Kay products, but she didn't make a great deal of money. Uncontrolled seizures were not acceptable in the 1950s for persons working in the education or therapeutic field. Although she had worked in banking, women were not allowed into the head offices of the bank when she began her apprenticeship in 1953 at $50 a month.

Her grandfather had left her money to take care of her medication, housing, and education in an attempt to make sure that she would always be able to obtain medication and live a reasonable quality of life. The stipulations in the trust were very strict and it could be administered only by a bank in Texas.

The state of Connecticut had tried unsuccessfully to find loop holes to break it when Emilia was still married to George and he was dealing with Title XIX or Medicaid, Reba had swindled them out of money twice, with Emilia's help, but this last time, she had said NO loud and clear.

Emilia didn't like having to depend on the trust, and as long as she and George had been married, she really had not used it very much. Neither of her sons-in-laws made much money, as both had physical problems that precluded their working. So there wasn't a great deal of money coming to Emilia from her children. Nicole had never married, and she had been off drugs since 1997 when she and her daughter Moona had moved in with Emilia and RC, the dog. She had paid a set amount while she lived there, but it barely covered their expenses. After they had sold George's car, Emilia resumed renting her garage at a modest sum of $50.00 to add to the treasury. George's alimony check had made the difference. When that was gone, there was a definite need to conserve on all expenditures.

That had been one reason that when she went back to school in 2007, she opted for student loans rather than getting the money from the trust. Emilia wanted the trust to go on to the next generation and then the next. She believed if it were placed with a bank again, it would grow. The recession that hit in 2008 was hurting the entire country. Although the TV and Radio Newscasters put a great deal of blame on the President, it was difficult to know if it was completely justified.

Emilia never forgot the story of Anne Vizisky, George's grandmother. She had refused to take welfare in 1929; instead she made paper flowers and sold them to put food on the table in South Dakota. Emilia wondered if people today had that kind of backbone and she prayed that they did. She knew the pitfalls of Medicare and Medicaid. She had watched the government take all of George's earnings, as well as those of an old friend from Minnesota, Andy Clark. When he had drowned in the 1990s, the state had taken everything. Andy, another epileptic who was never controlled, was said to have died in his bathtub because of a tonic-clonic seizure that went into status.

She had told Reba that all she wanted back was her mother's silver, her grandfather's clock and the $28,500.00 she had given her that was in an annuity that she had saved. It was her own money that she had saved from insurance payments and investment. She had held back $500, but the markets had reduced that to $250 by 2009.

In June of 2008, Emilia had confronted Reba over the phone and demanded the clock back. However, Reba contended that she couldn't remember where it was, and instead sent all of the silver back. Leah counted it piece by piece when it arrived shortly after her father's death.

Then, they considered going to Medford to look for things. But noone ever had time. By the time August 2008 came, Emilia was glad that she wasn't going to Cape Town for the IASSID congress. She wanted to stay in the Psychology program until she had completed it.

* * *

Section XII: 2009

Chapter XLII

Emilia sees doctor, has tests, studies and falls on ice

    In January Emilia met her new neurologist to get a second opinion. Nicole took her over to Milford to see the new doctor. After they got to the office, she didn't have long to wait before she was seen. Dr. Kong seemed like a thorough person. He talked to her and agreed to change the generic clonazepam back to the brand name Klonopin. He warned her that she might be sleepy, and she decided that she would only take it 3 times a day. Her former neurologist at Yale had told her to add an extra drug when she had more seizures. But during the fall, her seizures occurred at least three times a week, even with the increased dosage. She began taking the medication as soon as possible and found that her seizures reverted to those she had had in 1997. She was no longer plagued by confusion seizures, nor extensive walking seizures during which she had no memory of whom she was or what she was doing.

    Dr. Kong also ordered an EEG and an MRI to be done at Milford Hospital the following Monday. Emilia was impressed. Nicole had told her that she was chemically imbalanced, and she probably was. At least, with tests, which had not been done since 1997, they would have an idea of what problems were presently creating her seizures. At least she would get a second opinion.

    On the day that they went over to the hospital, Emilia took Nicole out for breakfast, as it was her birthday. At the hospital Emilia was surprised by the sounds that the MRI machine made. She hadn't remembered these same sounds in 1997. Perhaps the machine was newer or different. When she got home, after the EEG, she had to wash her hair to get the solution out of her hair. She was relieved that the wax came right out and wasn't the type that hardened and had to be taken out with alcohol. Over the years, she had seen many types of EEGs, and this one was fast and painless.

Snow and cold weather continued in January. After putting money in the bank and shopping at the Hong Kong Grocery Store, to her dismay she had one seizure in the grocery store, and another waiting for the bus. These were just seizures that prevented her from talking legibly and interfered with her memory. They did not confuse her. She still knew who she was. That was wonderful.

Forty-five minutes later, she caught the bus home. As she got off, the cell phone rang. Reaching to get it, she dropped her fruit on the cement, picking it up as she answered, she walked towards her home. The sun had come out. Suddenly, she stepped on ice and went down on her left hip. She told her granddaughter to keep talking to her and she slowly lay back in the snow to see if she could move. Yes, she could move, but it hurt. She rolled over, still talking and told Sheana to call her mother, or Nicole and then call her back. Sheana was more upset than Emilia who had gotten up, continued to talk and realized her beret wasn't on her head. She got up and walked, as the bone specialist in Minnesota had told her she should do if this happened. She walked up and down looking for the beret for about 20 minutes. Then, she decided to stop and rest. Leaning up against the building, she told Sheana that she was going to stop and wait for Nicole who was on the way.

As soon as she stopped, her head felt cold. She pulled the hood up, and there on her head was the beret, safely tucked inside the hood. Emilia was relieved, although she was sore. Leah had told her to walk on home, but she didn't want to walk forty feet or more on snow that might have turned to ice again; so she had decided to go to the hospital.

Isaiah, Moona's boyfriend, was driving when they got there. He was tall, and put out his elbow for Emilia to grab. She leaned against him, and hoped that her leg would not buckle as it had earlier.

When they got to the hospital, she was seen fairly quickly. She went for X-rays and was told that nothing was broken, nor was any hardware disturbed. The in-charge doctor told her to call her bone specialist in the next week or two. She said that she had Ibuprofen at home for pain. He suggested Tylenol for pain, but did not prescribe anything. Leah came by and told her that she would meet her at home. Isaiah and Moona had gone to Bridgeport so Isaiah could get a haircut. Emilia had only known that he was getting his hair cut and would be back shortly. After waiting an hour or more, Emilia was tired, sore and wet. About 4:00 p.m. they finally left the hospital. The skirt that she had on when she fell in the snow had dried a little on the cart when she was getting the X-rays, but not much.

Moona brought her something to eat. They still had her fruit in the car. Nicole did take one kiwi with her, but they had ordered her to eat nothing before the x-ray which had been about 1:30 or so.

After everyone had left, Pepper had been taken outside, and his mess cleaned up. Emilia struggled to get up, and wobbled to the bathroom. She took her clothes off and washed them in the kitchen, and hung them in the dining room and bathroom as usual. Then she took a sponge bath, and crawled into bed on the side nearest the door—the side that she used to sleep on. Tonight it felt good. She was out cold at 6 pm. She slept till the cell phone woke her up and she assured Nicole that she was OK. She asked her to call back at 11 pm. Then she took her meds and went back to sleep. She slept on the same side the next day as well. There were shooting pains in her leg, but the doctor had told her it was either a tendon or a muscle. Emilia knew that these muscle tares would be painful for a long time. She had had her share of falls. At 11 p.m., she took one Ibuprofen and that was all. The next morning she took a second. After that, she decided she could manage without them.

For the next fourteen days she stayed in bed and wrote or painted. Before she had gone to bed that day, she had gotten up and worked on the computer and sent in material for her homework that she had done the previous day.

She had planned to go to New York for the New York City Ballet on Sunday, but by Saturday she gave up the idea because she was moving less and less. She got up and ate and fed the dog on a regular basis. On Saturday, Leah had come over and given her a bath, washed her clothes, and changed the bed linens. She had also washed her hair. Emilia felt better after that.

She left word on Jana's answering machine that she had fallen, and she called back a few days later to see how she was. Jana was working in the school system and was busy with several jobs—playing in the church band, teaching music, teaching language, and selling Mary Kay cosmetics.

Emilia got into a new habit of working on a manuscript that she had been writing for 4 years at least twice a week, painting and working on the psychology course she was taking. This allowed her to lie flat on her back more often, which seemed to be the position that worked best for her leg. Her hip wasn't sore, it was the entire leg.

She had noticed that she wasn't as anxious as she used to be. Her appetite increased and food tasted better—a plus in her opinion.

Two weeks after her fall, she went shopping with Leah. Simon had fallen also on a computer and cut his forehead above his left eye. He stayed at home with Pepper, while they shopped. That night she had felt tired, but well. The following day, she took a bath when she discovered that she could stand without her cane without probability of falling.

Although she had missed the first ballet, she had intended to go to the second, however the weather was continuing cold and ice was everywhere. Emilia thought that she could ride the train into New York, but she wasn't sure about the shuttle underground, or the bus. Either option would require climbing and walking fast. She could walk, but not fast. The other problem would be the seat itself. There was little room and her legs would have to stay bent. What if she couldn't move when it was time to get up? She decided that maybe the ticket could be returned Monday, that would be soon enough as the ballet was the 15th of February. Time was flying by. There was only one week and two days left in this class. She had ordered the book for the class that began next, and hoped that it got there soon. It was on back-order, but if not, she would have to download and print it off. Time would tell. Physiological Behavior sounded like an interesting course to end on

* * *

Emilia went back to see Dr. Kong in February. He gave her a copy of the MRI, and talked to her about the findings of the MRI. He was relieved to know that the reason that her brain looked atrophied was because of the abuse that George had dealt her. He commented that it looked like the brain of a boxer. However, he considered her brain quite healthy. He was excited about the fact that she was completing her Masters in Psychology in March and wanted to continue on and write and teach about epilepsy.

Dr. Kong asked her to make an appointment to see him in three months time, which she did. In April, she began to question if she should contact him because her seizures had increased in number. Part of it was just being around people who put her under pressure. Another reason for the increase in seizures was one missed dose of both Klonopin and

Mebaral. It took her two weeks to get over that missed dose. Gradually, things seemed to calm down. In early March, she purchased a new printer, which scanned, copied and sent faxes. It didn't work for her until she had completed all of her coursework. Then she printed out 50 pages and had to buy new ink. It would be April before Moona had time to come over again and put the ink in for her and help her learn how to operate the new machine.

The day before Easter, Emilia decided that in December she would seek a PhD in Health Science in Psychology. This program included both statistical courses and neuroscience and would allow her to gain the background that she needed to continue to write. As strongly as she wished to improve the understanding and acceptance of persons with epilepsy within society, she knew that it would be an uphill battle. A PhD would give her words more credence, and enable her to teach as well.

*   *   *

In February, she had signed a contract for the new book. Then she began to write in earnest. By April 12th, she had the book compiled and was only waiting for the final chapter to unfold.

Chapter XLIII

*Moona considers her pregnancy and Isaiah.
Emilia entertains guests and works*

Moona was late beginning the course in nursing that she had hoped to take in high school. It would allow her to work as a nurses' assistant when she graduated in June. She believed Isaiah would be a good father. She liked his family because they made her feel accepted. Everyone was happy in the family.

Moona wasn't certain how her grandmother Gigi really felt about her pregnancy. When Emilia had told her granddaughter that she wasn't surprised that she was pregnant, Moona was shocked. Emilia had quickly added that she understood Moona because they were alike in many ways. Emilia reminded her that she had had desires at that age, but no-one was interested in her.

Gigi loved Moona unconditionally. Sometimes she would call and just tell her she loved her. That was Gigi. She seemed happier now that she was broke, and on new medication. Emilia was making good grades in graduate school. One thing about her grandmother, she did not give up. Neither did Moona. When Isaiah couldn't get work, Moona had found a job at a computer store and worked there as well as gone to school. She didn't quit until mid April and when the baby was born, she knew she had a job to which she could return. In 2009, many people were not as lucky.

Moona knew that her aunt and grandmother were glad that Sheana was going to college. She hoped that her cousin would do well in college and became a doctor's assistant. Shucks, she wanted everyone to be happy doing what they enjoyed. Wasn't that what life was all about, being happy?

Happiness hadn't been easy to come by for Moona. She smiled a lot, but there was a side of her that few people knew. She still couldn't understand why the man her mother said was her father wouldn't claim her as his daughter.

Uncle Theo was in his 40s before he found out who his father really was. She hoped that before she was 40 her father would show some interest in her. Next June she would be 19, still a child according to the insurance companies, but she would also be a mother. The word mother sounded good. Today, she and Auntie and Isaiah and her cousin Arnold had bought 20 different outfits for the baby daughter she was carrying.

The following week, Emilia was invited to the baby shower. She had completed the blue baby blanket that she had knitted, and Isaiah and Moona liked it. Everyone there seemed to enjoy themselves. Sheana was a little uneasy about selling Mary Kay but that was OK. She'd be fine, Emilia prayed.

* * *

A week or so later, Emilia had to exchange her printer, and then figure out how to work it. It took a while, but the new printer-fax-scanner-and copier worked well. Emilia found a high-chair near her friends' house. It was free, and in good condition. She called Nicole to ask if they had one. Nicole said "No." By that time Emilia had the high-chair at the front door. She got it inside, and thought that if Moona didn't use it someone would. Her leg was sore again because she had fallen when she reached for the high-chair that had collapsed.

In February, her neighbor began walking Pepper for her. She enjoyed the outings and the two canines became an item in the neighborhood. This had showed the world that Pepper could behave and have friends. Emilia had had an opportunity to have a break from walking him. Both were important to Emilia.

When Emilia's friend Jay came in town for a few days to visit, she had friends over and for once in a very long time, she felt as though other people around her did care what happened to her. Jay had her own set of physical problems, but like Emilia she worked out the problems and kept on going. Since she had retired from the Social Security Department in Minneapolis, she knew a lot of the legal ins and outs that Emilia didn't understand. After about four days, Jay returned home, having been away for over a week before she arrived at Emilia's. Jay was very active in the Order of the Eastern Star, and this gave her an outlet that kept her involved with other people. They had started a Navy Wives Club together in Bloomington when Emilia had lived there. After they turned it over to the new people, it folded.

* * *

Emilia had decided earlier in April to attend the 9th International Child Neurology Congress in Kiev in September. She had purchased tickets through her usual travel agent earlier in the month and made reservations at a hotel. All that needed to be done was payment of the registration fee. At this point, she was still waiting on the information from the Ukraine to find where to send the Euros.

Her seizures were lighter and didn't occur as often, but she now got more headaches than before. It was hard to tell whether the culprit was increased computer use, or the medication. Emilia was happy that her Mary Kay sales seemed on a rise. She needed to send out products today or tomorrow. Emilia began to plan ways to finance her PhD. Now that she had met with one of the teachers, she was excited about getting the program started. It would necessitate her going to Minneapolis and Dallas for 6 days in the next four years and that would enable her to see her daughter Yenta and their family. Life was good.

* * *

Get Published, Inc!
Thorofare, NJ 08086
14 April, 2010
BA2010104